Praise for *Into the Heart of Mindfulness*

'Mindfulness can transform suffering into compassion and joy and impact some of the problems we see in our world in a myriad of positive ways. However, to do this requires a deep understanding of mindfulness practice, ardency, courage and, frankly hard work over time. In *Into the Heart of Mindfulness* Ed Halliwell embodies everything he writes about, he 'walks the talk.' The fruits of this work for his own well-being, his family and the broader societal impact of his work are evident. This is one of the most substantial treatises on the transformative power of mindfulness written to date in contemporary times.'

Willem Kuyken, Professor and Director,
Oxford University Mindfulness Centre

'Open-hearted, honest and powerfully convincing, *Into the Heart of Mindfulness* is both a skilful guide to practice and a mirror into the stresses that bring us to seek greater mindfulness. Ed Halliwell's clear voice rises strongly from his own experience, pointing the way to peace of mind. This book is a great contribution to the field of secular contemplative practice.'

Sharon Salzberg, author of
Lovingkindness and *Real Happiness*

'Ed shows us in a remarkably moving way how mindfulness worked for him. And then he shows how it can also work for millions of others who seek a calmer, deeper mode of life.'

Lord Richard Layard, Professor of Economics and Head of
Well-Being programme at London School of Economics, author
of *Happiness* and *Thrive*, co-founder of Action for Happiness

'Using his own movingly honest ⸻⸻ ⸻⸻ ⸻al struggle with suffering, Ed Hal ⸻⸻ ⸻⸻ hrough the transformative potentia ⸻⸻ ⸻⸻ ing on the Buddhist foundations o ⸻⸻ ⸻⸻ the recent scientific research into i ⸻⸻ ⸻⸻ indfulness approach that moves fai ⸻⸻ ⸻⸻ ⸻unded and hopeful path towards wholehearted engagement with life.'

Robert Marx, Consultant Clinical Psychologist,
Lead for Mindfulness Training and Governance,
Sussex Partnership NHS Foundation Trust

'Ed Halliwell's *Into the Heart of Mindfulness* stands out in the increasingly crowded field of mindfulness literature. If you are looking for a practical manual with meditation exercises, a lucid account of Buddhist psychology, insights from the cutting-edge of scientific research, as well as a moving personal story, this is the mindfulness book for you.'

Stephen Batchelor, author of
After Buddhism: Rethinking the Dharma for a Secular Age

'With this book Ed Halliwell confirms his place as one of the most insightful and authentic voices in the mindfulness movement. The book is both a riveting personal memoir and a map of the human mind which we all share. Ed writes vividly and honestly about his own experience of depression, and how mindfulness has helped him to enjoy life again. He interweaves this narrative with an explanation of mindfulness training and how it functions, exploring the workings of the mind and emotions with clarity and depth. This book will surely inspire many readers to look beyond clichés about mindfulness, and perhaps to take the first steps of a lifelong journey.'

Tessa Watt, author of *Mindful London* and
Introducing Mindfulness: A Practical Guide

'Ed has written a remarkable book. With great insight, heart and knowledge, he shows us the light at the end of the long dark tunnel of depression – that light is mindfulness meditation. Weaving his personal experience with the scientific evidence, and some thoughtful mindfulness exercises for the reader to try, Ed gives a convincing account of how mindful being in this world changes our relationship with ourselves and others, moving from individual development to becoming a social force. Read his book, put it aside and sit in silence. Breathe the difference!'

Dr Florian Ruths, Consultant Psychiatrist and Clinical Lead for
Mindfulness-based Therapy, South London and Maudsley NHS Trust

'Searingly honest, tender and wise. If you were to read just a few of the many mindfulness books out there, make sure you read this one. Ed Halliwell has masterfully created a book that shares his own journey through the demons of anxiety and depression and into the heart of mindfulness. It is a brilliant translation of the deeper traditions of Buddhism for the modern reader. One of the best mindfulness books I have read.'

Vidyamala Burch, co-founder of Breathworks and co-author
of *Mindfulness for Health* and *Mindfulness for Women*

into the Heart of Mindfulness

Finding a Way of Well-being

ED HALLIWELL

piatkus

PIATKUS

First published in Great Britain in 2016 by Piatkus

1 3 5 7 9 10 8 6 4 2

A CIP catalogue record for this book
is available from the British Library.

ISBN 978-0-349-40671-8

Typeset in Swift by M Rules
Printed and bound in Great Britain by
Clays Ltd, St Ives plc

Papers used by Piatkus are from well-managed forests
and other responsible sources.

MIX
Paper from
responsible sources
FSC® C104740

Piatkus
An imprint of
Little, Brown Book Group
Carmelite House
50 Victoria Embankment
London EC4Y 0DZ

An Hachette UK Company
www.hachette.co.uk

www.improvementzone.co.uk

About the author

Ed Halliwell is a mindfulness teacher and writer. He is the author of *Mindfulness: How To Live Well by Paying Attention* and co-author of *The Mindful Manifesto: How Doing Less and Noticing More Can Help Us Thrive in a Stressed-Out World*. Ed leads public mindfulness courses and workshops in London and Sussex, and has introduced and taught mindfulness in many businesses, schools and charities. He is on the faculty of the School of Life, and is an advisor to, and former co-director of, The Mindfulness Initiative, which is supporting the Mindfulness All-Party Parliamentary Group to develop mindfulness-based policies for the UK. He also wrote the Mental Health Foundation's *Be Mindful Report*, which spearheaded an influential campaign to bring mindfulness training into the NHS.

For Vicki and the boys.
For my family. And for everyone
touched by suffering.
May we all know contentment and
the roots of contentment.

Contents

Preface

A few years ago, mindfulness meditation went largely unnoticed by mainstream society. Likely to be thought of as something done by Buddhists, or perhaps an 'alternative' health technique for new-age types, it wasn't widely seen as having a role in fields such as medicine, education, politics or business. Many people would have considered it a bit weird.

All this has changed, and quickly. Thanks to the development and spread of mainstream courses, which teach meditation as part of a non-religious approach to well-being, and a growing evidence base that suggests a range of positive effects on human flourishing, mindfulness has sprung up seemingly everywhere. It is discussed and practised not just in healthcare settings but as a way to wise living in schools, workplaces and even in government. As speed and stress seem ever more endemic, a method that invites stillness, awareness, presence and compassion perhaps no longer looks so strange. We are in desperate need of ways to manage our lives and world.

The benefits of mindfulness rest on the paradox that well-being comes when we let go of battling for it. Mindfulness practice helps us see that grasping for pleasure and running from pain actually lead to discontent. It invites us to understand and unhook from the craving, clinging and aversion that fuel our compulsive search for happiness, and instead connect with life as it is. Things start to shift when we drop the drive to be rid of stress.

This approach goes against the grain. Our minds, bodies and environments are geared to push for pleasure and get away from misery. The idea seems obvious that if we want to be happy, we should hold tightly to what we like and ward off what we don't like. It can be most perplexing as we try to get to grips with a method that shows us this view is delusional and that a life based on it is unsatisfactory. And as soon as we grip, it is no longer mindfulness.

Nevertheless, if we give ourselves to the practice, things can make sense. Tuning to the truths of life, and acting from what we find, we discover wisdom in this way. When we enjoy the world's wonders without trying to own them – and work with its stresses rather than shun them – we start to lead a more liberated life. Being *with* experience, rather than reacting *against* it, we lay the ground for good choices.

Very few of us get this easily. I know I don't. Especially at first, we can sometimes mistake mindfulness for a strategy to shut off from fear, dislike and discomfort, or to protect us from pain, uncertainty and sadness – a supposed quick fix for all our ills. These misunderstandings are normal, because we inevitably bring to the training our habitual patterns of mind, and those of our world. So, it helps to explore this way in depth, with support, and repeatedly. This invites mindfulness, not just as a short course or good idea but as a sustained, sustaining way to live. Our habitual patterns are strong, but by gently marinating our minds, bodies and lives in the practice, we can begin to be free.

Meditation transforms unskilful habits by inviting us to see them and by helping shift our relationship to them. By coming back to our senses, back to awareness, again and again, we infuse our minds, bodies and behaviour with presence. In the embodiment of mindfulness practice, we uncover the capacity to live with gentleness, kindness and equanimity. As we let the approach soak in, the effects start to show. We may still take action, but no longer in such a frenzied state.

This has been my experience. Having come to meditation in a desperate bid to be rid of anxiety and depression, I was a walking example of how misery springs from struggle, over-thinking and rejection of pain. Gradually, however, my life has changed. Although I'm still prone to these patterns, I'm more able to unhook from them now. My relationship with old habits has shifted as I've become more aware of them, and friendlier towards them. Over time, I've come to appreciate these tendencies – and everything else in life – as impermanent and insubstantial processes, rather than fixed essences. This has led to a gentler, more flexible, resilient way of being, in my mind and body. As the relationship with my inner world has changed, life has flowed in a happier direction.

I've shared some of my experience in this book. By telling this story, I hope it will become clear that while mindfulness has had a profound effect on my life, it has been no quick fix. Change has come gradually, with many obstacles along the way. Ultimately, however, it seems the extent of my contentment depends on the capacity – deepened through practice – to slow down and open myself not just to pleasure and ease but also to stress and difficulty. The more I've continued, the more I've found that freedom emerges from meeting and befriending life's troubles, rather than resisting them.

In our desire to make things easier, we may shy away from the challenges of practice – moving towards difficulty, working with impermanence, accepting limitation. However, great rewards can come from bringing mindfulness to the *whole* of life, including – *especially* – its less palatable parts. This is the heart of the way, which is the way of the heart – indeed, mindfulness connects us to *our* hearts, to *our* wholeness. If we can give ourselves to it fully, over and over with tenderness, courage and patience, we discover a wealth that already exists in our mind, body and world, but which we miss in our futile, frenetic striving for fast and simple routes to pleasure. With an extended, loving embrace we can rediscover life as a deeply nourishing, multi-textured, *heartfelt* experience, the beauty and wonder of which does not depend on everything going our way. By journeying into this heart of mindfulness, we instigate a peaceful revolution in our lives.

If this kind of engagement is realised, as mindfulness spreads to the mainstream, it could bring about a much-needed shift. As we open up to our shared heart, our mutual dependency, we are inevitably drawn to expand the practice into the realm of community. We come to understand that true well-being cannot be found in isolation. Seeing how we affect and are affected by the wider world, we realise that contentment comes only by working together. Entering the heart of mindfulness thus means opening to and working with both inner depth and outer breadth, through quiet contemplation, warm-hearted connection *and* constructive action, usually in that order. With this as our anchor and compass, we could be on course for healthier, happier lives in a healthier, happier world.

In an attempt to express this fully, I begin this book with my own journey, before expanding outwards. The first chapters describe my experience with depression and anxiety, and what happened when I began to meditate. Next, I look at how mindfulness has come to reach many more people, mainly through the work of scientists and clinicians who have taught and researched it in a mainstream framework. I outline some core learnings of a mindfulness course, and explain how these invite awareness and attunement. I've highlighted challenging parts of the training, which can get glossed over in cursory guides, and which take us into the core of the practice, offering a rich and deep experience that goes beyond a typical search for happiness. Finally, I explore how mindfulness can bring appropriate action, not as a frantic struggle for betterment, but as an organic outcome of awareness, presence and kindness. Because the training points us to a skilful relationship with our inner and outer world, I suggest this also leads to a greater care for the people and environment around us. Thus it sparks potential for a wider movement to well-being, found and practiced collectively. Throughout the book, I include guidance on some of the core practices that might inspire these changes.

Mindfulness *can* help us find happiness. However, we may need to alter our view of happiness, and prepare to live life in a rather unusual way.

I hope you enjoy the book, and that it proves helpful.

CHAPTER ONE

Only Half-Awake

Compared with what we ought to be,
we are only half-awake.

William James[1]

Thigh muscles throbbing. Stomach somersaulting. Shoulders locked. Fingers quivering. Feet twitching. Teeth clenched tight. Pressure in the bridge of the nose. Hot and cold simultaneously behind the eyes. Pangs of panic gripping the chest, heart pulsing fast and hard. Anger, like a scream bellowing out from the midriff. A shield of hard depression encasing the skin, walling off the body from the outside world. Thoughts circling round and round, the same ruminations over and over again: 'Why am I stuck like this? Is it ever going to end? Why can't I be more like other people? Why can't I cope? What's wrong with me? I hate this, I hate this. I'm scared, *still* scared after all this time. This is never going to work. I am *never* going to get better. It's useless. Useless. *Useless!*'

I'm learning to meditate. Perched atop a square, hard cushion in the corner of my bedroom, trying to pay attention to the movement of my breath, and *this* is what I'm noticing. It's the same kind of anguish that's accompanied every waking hour for the past two and a half years. The fear, the rage, the helplessness. But there's a subtle and crucial difference this time. I'm beginning to observe these patterns of thought and feeling from a different place, from somewhere I didn't previously know existed. Rather than feeling caught up entirely in the mental noise, the exhaustion, the tension, I'm beginning to *watch* what's happening. Perhaps not yet with equanimity – as is meant to be possible with enough practice – but at least without feeling that my life is nothing but pain. A sliver of space is opening up between 'me' and the tormenting thoughts and sensations that are surging through 'me'. Hmm, this is interesting . . .

Then – *bang!* I'm right back in it: 'You stupid idiot! You've lost it. You'll never be able to do this properly. It's a waste of time. You're sitting doing nothing when you should be sorting your life out. Ow, ow, ow, my head hurts, my legs ache, and as for my stomach . . . Oh, stop it, please stop it, I can't stand this any longer. It's not fair. *Why* is this still happening to me?'

All right, hold on a minute. What am I supposed to be doing? I'm meant to label it, right? Okay. 'Thinking'. It's thinking. Not facts, just thinking. Let it be. Come back to the breath. The mind is wandering. No problem. Just bring it back gently. I can do this. I *am* doing it. Following the breath in, then out, in, out. Let thoughts and feelings do whatever they want. I don't have to try to make them go away. It's okay.

Bang! Once again, the gentle voice is drowned out by the goading of my old tormenter. 'Oh come on! You don't believe this stuff works, do you? You'll never change. This is who you are. This has been going on for years, so why would meditation help when nothing else has. You're wasting your time. It's another fad. This is ridiculous. You're messed up, you're . . . '

Okay, drop it. It's still just *thinking*. Pause. Breathe. Now inhaling, now exhaling, back with the breath. It's okay. It's okay. It's okay. Just look; just watch. No big deal.

So here I am. Sitting on a cushion, following the breath, watching the crazy ruminations, allowing the tension, getting caught up and then letting go, again and again.

I've been practising for a couple of months now – daily doses of five or ten minutes, as agreed with my meditation teacher. Initially, even this seemed too much – the invitation to experience just a little stillness, and its implied tolerance of anxiety, was too overwhelming for me. So we started with mindful tea-drinking. My challenge was to drink one cup a day, paying attention to all the sensations of taste, touch and smell, and returning to these whenever I noticed my mind descend into tangles of thought, as it desperately tried to crack the problem of 'What is happening to me and why? And what can I possibly do about it?'

What *was* happening to me? Before the depression set in, life had looked and felt pretty good. In my mid-twenties, I had been deputy editor of one of the best-selling magazines in Europe, having graduated with flying colours from what is generally regarded as a top university. I had good friends, sometimes girlfriends, and the kind of lifestyle that many people my age would have envied. I worked long hours, but that included travelling to fancy hotels in exotic locations to organise photo shoots, attending parties with complimentary drinks, interviewing actors and actresses, sports stars and musicians, and coming up with ideas for stupid stories to amuse young men. Then, between games of pool, I'd commission writers to draft the features that my colleagues and I had dreamed up on a whim – whatever tickled our cynical and deprecating senses of humour.

This was the late 1990s, when men's lifestyle magazines were at the height of their popularity, and there was a kind of unthinking fun to be had by those who worked on them. But while the free clothes and watches, the glamour and the prestige, the careless laughter, the buzz of thrill-seeking all satisfied a certain shallow craving for pleasure, under the surface my life was not so enjoyable. I had a series of romantic relationships, but they rarely lasted more than a few months. I had a seemingly fabulous career, but it masked an undercurrent of yearning for something more, although I had no idea what that something might be. I frequently batted away feelings of hollowness and melancholy, as well as vague premonitions of a fearful future. I was lonely, and when the parties ended I'd try to keep the worry away by playing myself at darts, drinking vodka and spacing out with Sky Sports News on the TV. But the more I tried to fill the days and nights with pleasure, the more the darkness loomed at the edges of my mind. Questions about the meaning of existence started to creep in, accompanied by nervous rumblings in my gut, especially during rare moments of quiet, which I tried to keep to a minimum.

Frightened of silence, I surrounded myself with noise. Frightened of change, I worked hard at a lifestyle that lacked the lively curiosity I'd nurtured through my university days. Finding a harsh outside world when I left the academic cocoon, I reacted by shutting down feelings and becoming hard of heart. Frightened of being hurt by others, I no longer shared any sense of vulnerability. Instead, I threw myself into ever more frantic activity, be it buying clothes, going to the gym or creating dramas with girlfriends. Or I'd try to dull the unease by drinking alcohol or smoking dope.

I seemed to function well enough most of the time, surviving on the surface. Only a few times did the veneer crack, usually after a girlfriend's rejection. Whenever this happened, anger and fear would shoot through my body, along with the sudden racing of a mind yelping from hurt, desperately searching for an exit from suffering. This sudden and scary automatic reaction would usually last for a few weeks or months, during which time I would barely eat or sleep, consumed by obsessive thoughts about how to put things right. The volcano of emotion would eventually subside, sometimes as a result of a new relationship, or by resurrecting the old one. Or there might be another form of distraction – perhaps a promotion or a holiday in the sun.

But the patch jobs and distractions ultimately failed to do the trick. Soon after the millennium turned, another fledgling relationship came to an abrupt end, and this time my escape tactics couldn't divert me from the pain. There was no one new on the horizon. Attempts to throw myself into work projects didn't satisfy: the conveyor belt of gadgets, models and puerile jokes was starting to lose its appeal – something in me called for an engagement of heart. A comfortable flat share with an old friend was also coming to an end, and I was secretly scared of living alone.

Loss of girlfriend, loss of companionship, loss of professional identity. Combined, it all felt too much to bear. It was like I'd been strapped to an out-of-control helicopter: my stomach lurched up and down as catastrophic thoughts ('You're going mad. This is a disaster . . .') rattled through my head in a crazed, repeating loop. Muscles were frozen in terror, fingers trembled, and my breath hardened to a shallow pant.

Seeing no way out, I collapsed. Or rather, the rickety façade that I thought was 'me' collapsed. After several weeks at work trying to pretend everything was fine, I called in sick, unable to face another week of going to the bathroom every twenty minutes to cry, fruitlessly berating myself to 'get it together'. At home, things only got worse. Now I had all day to lie in bed or pace up and down, fretfully running through what was going wrong and how I might put it right. I passed the time chain-smoking (another futile diversion technique) and calling friends, family and even the Samaritans, hoping someone might offer an antidote to the poison that was eating me. Was I suicidal? No, but I desperately wanted the pain to stop.

It didn't stop for quite a while. I moved into a new flat and, as expected, felt very lonely in it. I sobbed myself to sleep on many nights (on the others, my brain just whirred and whirred until unconsciousness came as precious relief). After several months off work, and still unable to face a return to the office, I went freelance, basing myself at home (and thus deepening the isolation and loneliness). I made a living, but found no joy in the work.

All I could really focus on was the depression. I went on a frantic quest to discover the cause of my symptoms, and how to be rid of them. The first stop was my GP. 'I'm having a breakdown,' I told him. 'My girlfriend left me, I'm in the wrong job, I'm scared to live alone and I can't stop crying. All I can think about is how terrible everything is and I can't eat or sleep. Please help me.'

'You're upset,' he replied softly. 'I'll give you some antidepressants, but what'll really help is counselling. It sounds like you've been shoving everything under the carpet and that's not working any more.'

'Yes,' I replied meekly. 'But now what?'

'You have to start looking at what's under the carpet. Counselling will help you to do that.'

Before I left my job, I'd been invited to see an occupational coach who was also a psychotherapist – the company agreed to pay for a few meetings. I learned a lot during the sessions about the workings of my mind. I realised I wanted to be seen as successful, attractive and clever, and came to understand that this self-image was held in place by a range of circumstantial props, such as job status, money, material possessions, and feeling wanted and loved in a romantic relationship. This seemed like useful information, and the counselling provided a supportive way of processing it, so when my employers' funding ran out, I paid for more sessions out of my own pocket. Yet no matter how much I talked, reflected, probed and analysed (and I did a lot of all four), I still felt no better. After two years of traipsing in and out of the consulting room, I was just as miserable as before.

Why wasn't the therapy shifting my gloom? With hindsight, it's clear that while I grew familiar with what wasn't working, I didn't learn the skills to untangle myself from it. My therapist suggested that I 'over-identified with emotions'. Actually, I over-identified with *everything*: thoughts, feelings, people, work, property, clothes. Life – in terms of the things I desired *and* the things from which I wanted to escape – weighed heavily on me. Yet, the more I focused on the problem, the worse it became. No matter how hard I tried, I couldn't seem to change.

No matter how hard I tried …

And I was trying very, very hard. Within weeks of starting therapy, one wall of my bedroom was stacked waist high with psychology and self-help books. Among many other topics, I was reading up on how to forge a successful relationship (*Women who Love too Much*, *Games People Play*), manage mental states and emotions (*Feel the Fear and Do It Anyway*, *I'm Okay, You're Okay*), be more purposeful (*The Seven Habits of Highly Effective People*), understand the past and its effects on the psyche (the works of Freud, Jung and Winnicott) and explore spirituality (*The Tibetan Book of Living and Dying*). Several times each week I attended meetings of Co-Dependents Anonymous and other 'twelve-step' groups that focused on addiction to relationships. I was also working my way through a chemist's shelf of antidepressants, one brand after another. I tried alternative treatments like acupuncture and biodynamic massage, and toyed with lifestyle changes: should I move to Australia or perhaps share a flat again? Even my writing reflected this desperate, scattergun approach to life and recovery – as I searched for new paths, I wrote travel pieces, business analyses, book reviews, real-life stories, psychology features, confessionals, even an agony-uncle column.

It was a frantic search for contentment that must have been exhausting. But as I was already so very tired, I didn't notice how hard I was driving myself. My mind and body were stuck in a cycle of fear and regret, and I had lost all touch with the effects of my actions. I couldn't see that each time I rushed into the next support group, therapy session or self-help treatise, I was actually pushing away the peace I craved. I was trying to force myself into a future state of calm, but the forcing itself kept the tension in place. The more I tried to fight or run from fear and rumination, the more I fuelled a pattern of aversion, a hatred of the present that made me feel worse, impelling me to fight or run even more. No matter what I changed in my external life, no matter what I tried to change in my psyche, I remained stuck in a pattern of resistance to the moment. And just as that cycle of behaviour kept repeating, so did my cycle of experience. No matter what I tried, I woke up each morning and went to bed each night depressed, scared, frustrated and tired.

At times, from the outside, it would look like I was holding up. I managed to meet most of my deadlines, smile at interviewees and colleagues, pay the bills, and appear to enjoy playing football, watching a film or attending a party. At others, I couldn't find the energy to keep up appearances, and I would break down. Shattered from all the striving, and exasperated at finding it impossible to escape from misery, I'd drop into a wailing heap, crying impotent tears of rage. Other times I was so angry and dissociated that I couldn't cry. I'd just go to bed and lie there frozen, mummified by muscle tension, stuck in relentless thinking. Letters went unopened, dishes sprouted mould in the sink, and days went by as I hid from an outside world that rudely signalled its ongoing presence through shaking bedroom walls as lorries thundered past outside. I was often so lifeless I'd only make it to the fridge once or twice a day, surviving on the occasional can of beans, washed down with fruit juice. My weight yo-yoed. During the periods of mad activity, I'd shovel down a dozen bowls of cereal a day. Along with cigarettes, I used eating as a way to avoid feelings, and I quickly piled on the pounds. Then, in times of lethargy, I'd hardly eat and the weight would fall off. It was the same boom-and-bust pattern, written on my body, that played out in my psyche.

When nothing changed after days under the duvet, I'd eventually drag myself up, issuing mental threats to myself of house repossession or death from malnutrition. I'd grit my teeth, trudge to the shops for supplies, and get on the phone in the hunt for work. Or I'd start a new round of fruitless solution-seeking, ringing the surgery for an emergency appointment, or leaving a trail of messages for my therapist or the members of my latest support group: 'Help me, please help me. I think I might be dying. I can't do this any longer. Please help me *now*.'

When these pleas failed to generate an immediate response, I'd show up at yet another twelve-step meeting – in London, a new group seemed to launch every other week – and sit and listen to others' tales of struggle or recount my own, hoping for salvation through sharing stories. Occasionally, I'd make the trip to Accident and Emergency at the local hospital and demand to see a psychiatrist. The best they could usually offer was a friendly (or sometimes not-so-friendly) chat, another antidepressant prescription, and an explanation that I wasn't sufficiently ill to be admitted to a ward, which – they said – would probably make me worse anyway. On one occasion, I answered a straight-faced 'yes' to the question 'Are you suicidal?' as I knew that would leave them no option but to admit me. However, warnings about the dire state of the wards rang in my ears, and I bottled it at the last minute, changed my plea and begged to go home.

At my times of greatest despair, I leaned heavily on my family. I'd decamp for days, weeks or even months to my parents' house. Ostensibly, this was for rest and recuperation, but really it was a retreat into childhood. A long way from my own home, with no work or friends near by, I'd try to distract myself from the whirring of my mind by filling in crosswords. Once again, there were times when I never got out of bed. With no obligation to go to the shops for food (my poor parents – not knowing how to help – had issued assurances that they would never let me go homeless or hungry), I'd hole myself up in a bedroom until the isolation started to feel worse than the prospect of getting up. Finally, I'd crawl into the shower and try to face the world again. Each of my brothers and several friends also provided sanctuary at times. But I was hardly in a state to be supported: I was too closed down.

Deep in the depressive's cave, I could see the core problem and how it might be relieved. Before I started therapy, one of my brothers had given me a book on Taoist healing, which included advice on 'people-surfing', breathing and letting go. I was intrigued by these concepts as they seemed so far removed from how I lived my life, which was all about people-craving, breathlessness and holding on. The book recommended meditation as a means of Taoist training, and I intuitively felt this was important advice. But, although I grasped the idea (and appreciated the possible benefits), all I felt when I tried to meditate was a surging heart rate, a wrenching gut and mental spaghetti. Surely, this wasn't what was supposed to happen? Where was the promised relaxation? After a handful of one-minute sessions, I branded myself a meditation failure and gave up.

But as I continued to search for recovery, certain themes kept recurring in my reading and in suggestions from others: 'stop trying so hard', 'accept yourself', 'open up', 'allow yourself to feel'. To me, these were trite phrases that described experiences I'd never had and that I had little inkling of how to access. Before long, whenever someone told me to 'let go' or 'accept myself', I would answer with a glare. What do they even mean by 'let go'? How dare they offer such facile remedies for the excruciating pain I've endured for so long?

Truisms and self-help advice were getting my goat, but there was one view of my predicament that I couldn't fault. As I bounced from one set of supposed answers to the next (each time I finished a volume, I'd scan through the bibliography and order more), a certain way of seeing, being and acting started to make sense. Buddhism. In diagnosing the problem of human suffering, the Buddha offered a straightforward outline of the cause, an optimistic prognosis and a practical treatment plan. Humans experience stress, he explained, because we become attached. We want to be happy, to hold on to pleasure and to steer clear of pain. We want to feel permanent and secure. In a futile attempt to create happiness and security, we cast delusions on ourselves, others and the world around, believing at a deep emotional level that if we try hard enough, we will succeed in preventing the flow of change in life. We think, with sufficient effort, that all of our ducks can be set in a row. Unconsciously, through force of habit, we cling to people, possessions, substances and ideas, haplessly clutching at whatever straws seem to promise pleasure.

But the permanent pleasure we crave is a fantasy. Life can never be one long high. Rather, it is a dynamic journey through the 'ten thousand joys and ten thousand sorrows' – with death, another transition, waiting at the end. None of us wants it to be this way, so we reach out and grab for something else – *anything* else – that might return us to the safety of our illusions, to soothe our discomfort at the unpalatable truths of existence. This may work for a time, but only until the next awakening jolt – such as a sudden illness, redundancy, or the end of a relationship. Then, once again, the fantasy and the reality jar, leaving us reeling. And so it goes on – a constant struggle to avoid painful truths and grab pleasant illusions, a clinging to whatever objects of desire seem within reach, followed by inevitable suffering as those objects slip from our grasp, exposing us yet again to suffering.

This was precisely how I had lived my life. My attachments were indisputable. I was *desperate* for happiness, yet everything I did to achieve it ultimately threw me into turmoil. My apparently successful career had offered a temporary protective bubble, but the blissful ignorance had now been torn and there was nowhere to hide. I had fallen prey to what the Buddha called the 'Eight Worldly Concerns' (Praise and Blame, Gain and Loss, Fame and Disrepute, Pleasure and Pain), determined to secure the first of each pair and prevent the second. This pursuit had left me floundering in a self-sustaining eddy of stress – trying to find what I didn't have and trying to rid myself of what I didn't want. Grasp, run away, grasp, run away, grasp, run away. Buddhist terminology describes this as *samsara* – life's wheel of suffering.

The more I read of what the Buddha had taught, the more I felt a deep resonance. This wasn't something I had to 'believe'; it was what I already knew. Poring through Buddhist texts was like re-encountering maps of understanding I had lost and forgotten existed. Sure, there were elements of Buddhism that sounded like religion – suggesting what may happen beyond this life – but the core of its doctrine was immediately applicable to the here and now. *My* here and now.

What's more, there was a prescription to follow – and a seemingly simple one, too. In order to be free of suffering (the Buddha's first noble truth), one had to stop clinging (the second noble truth). This was exactly what everyone had been telling me – just let go. But the Buddha went further. Not only was this letting go possible (the third noble truth), but there was a path to achieve it – a 'how-to guide' – which came in the form of a clearly outlined set of instructions. Through cultivating skilful ways of living (right view, right intention, right speech, right action, right livelihood, right effort, right mindfulness, right concentration – the eightfold path), it was possible to free oneself from torment. We could – I could – be happy.

This prescription was different from all the others I had tried or studied. First, it was 2500 years old, so it had clearly stood the test of time. Moreover, despite the substantial claim that liberation was possible for everyone, it didn't have the odour of snake oil. The Buddha explained that the path can – and probably will – be difficult: our habits are tenacious, so it's not easy to let them go. Nevertheless, the Buddhist view is that we are deluded and unskilful, rather than intrinsically broken, so we are capable of change. It's really up to us. No god or higher power is required, although we must be willing to learn and practise, preferably under guidance and with support.

This does not mean contorting ourselves into a new shape. The Buddha's understanding was that a wise way of being can be found within each of us, beneath the cloak of illusion. The path is not about the attainment of goals, so much as about letting go of unhelpful habits, so a more harmonious relationship with life can unfold. We don't need to strain and push, hammering ourselves like a blacksmith working with iron; instead, we can connect to a wisdom that's already present, albeit obscured. Rather than trying to change our circumstances – which may not be feasible, and certainly isn't a lasting cure – we work to change our *relationship with* our circumstances. This enables us to perceive the world in a different way. As Marcel Proust put it: 'The only true voyage of discovery ... would be not to visit strange lands but to possess other eyes.'[2] In this analysis, I needed not so much a change of situation, but a change of heart.

If there was no need to strive for transformation, there was no need to struggle. Indeed, struggle, I learned, served only to block the path. If we focus continually on trying to create a better future, then we aren't in a good position to understand and relate well to the present (which, after all, is the only thing that is ever truly happening). Therefore, the first step on the journey is to explore carefully what's going on right now. And to do that, it's important to learn how to meditate. Mindfulness meditation, say Buddhists, is an essential tool for seeing the truth of what's happening, enabling us to develop the skills to free us from helpless habit, cultivating our capacity to live wisely.

So, painful though it promised to be, I vowed to try meditation again. Beginning on my own, using written instructions as a guide, I devoted five minutes or so each day to following my breathing. It was just as tortuous as before – every few seconds I would feel the urge to leap into (distr)action, anything to take me away from the agony of sitting quietly with mind–body turmoil. But as I gradually started to accept that there are no quick fixes, I began to give in to the process, allowing myself to experience, without resistance, the sensations and thoughts that were coursing through my body and mind. For these short periods of time, I bore witness to them, in spite of the flow of thoughts that continued to label the exercise pointless.

I was reminded of one of my early therapy sessions. Tangled up as usual in some mental drama with an ex-girlfriend, and flying into a panic over how this made me feel, the therapist had said: 'Ed, could you just observe the experience?'

'Could I *what*?'

'Observe the experience. Just watch what's happening, as if you're looking in from outside. Be interested in what's happening – what you're thinking, how you're feeling.'

I found this idea somewhat mind-blowing – even the possibility that I could do such a thing. But on my journey home to Battersea, clambering aboard a bus, I dutifully tried to 'observe my experience'. And you know what, I managed it ... for a while. I watched myself pay for a ticket and talk to the driver. I noticed the feeling on the soles of my feet as they walked to the upper deck. I saw myself sitting down and looking at the people below. I looked at my thoughts: the stream of raging, whining thoughts that were cascading through my head. I saw my body – its locked-in, tight rigidity (clenched teeth and jaw, hunched shoulders) and restlessness (trembling hands and knees, tumbling gut). And, for the first time ever, it struck me – *all this stuff that's going on inside me isn't actually me*. Or, at least, it isn't the *whole* of me. If it were, how would I be able to watch it like this? So what – or who – is watching? Hmm, curious.

The semi-mystical bus experience was over in a matter of minutes, but I remembered the flash of insight and the warm feeling it produced, even though I never managed to replicate it through conscious effort. Later, as I began to practise meditation, every so often it would happen again – a momentary glimmer of an experience that was bigger than my pain, a little space around the crush of distress. Something told me I was on the right track, but I knew I couldn't go very far on my own. Surfing the web for suitable support, I saw there was a Buddhist centre ten minutes' walk from my house. Gathering all my courage, I decided to pay it a visit.

So began my mindful tea-drinking.

Recognising that her student was extremely stressed, my first instructor proposed a very gentle regime. I followed it to the letter and, for the first time since I had toppled into depression, felt like something might be shifting. The gloom didn't lift immediately, but I could sense that my mindset was starting to move. Instead of always trying to improve a situation through struggle or avoidance, I began to understand that there was possibly no need for so much to happen. Maybe my challenge was not to push with grit and determination, but to learn to *be with* whatever was happening – to allow anxiety, helplessness and racing thoughts, rather than try to shove them out of consciousness. This still seemed a tall order, but 'letting be' and 'acceptance' were no longer entirely alien concepts. I experienced little glimmers of them during meditation.

And so I continued, first with more mindful cups of tea, then with two, five, ten or even sometimes fifteen minutes of sitting each day. I tried to allow whatever thoughts and feelings were present, using the breath as an anchor to which I could return, whenever the mind wandered off. I tried to remember that there was no goal, so it was impossible to fail. All I had to do was keep returning to the breath, with gentleness and patience, noticing what was happening without making judgements, seeing the experience as neither good nor bad.

Every other approach I'd tried had seemed to be about someone offering a fix or about me learning how to repair myself. Here, the view was that nothing was really wrong, so there was no problem to be sorted out. At worst, I was merely confused about how to live well; and the first step out of that confusion was to realise how it functioned, through the practice of mindfulness meditation.

I could manage this for a few minutes each day. But the rest of my life was still manic. I was scooting from support group to support group, frantically jumping from one assignment to the next, trying geographical cures (a new rented office was the latest attempt to find some company) and analysing my life to death in therapy. I was still latched on to a range of self-diagnosed psychiatric conditions – one week I was a relationship addict, the next bipolar, then an obsessive–compulsive, and after that I had generalised anxiety disorder. Each, of course, had its own treatment regime, and my vain hope was that if I could make the correct diagnosis, recovery would follow. The Buddha's diagnosis – that I was a normal human being experiencing normal human suffering (and reacting to it unskilfully) – was certainly appealing. But his meditative medicine seemed too slow whenever I spiralled into another frenzy.

In the summer of 2003, I started work as a volunteer in a charity's press office. This was my latest wheeze – redemption through ethical employment. As usual, I dived in head-first, working like crazy to make a mark. And, as usual, it didn't work. Although it looked like I'd be offered a job, I was going home at the end of each day and falling straight into bed, exhausted by the stress of appearing calm in the exposed environment of an open-plan office. I was almost back at square one, toughing it out in the workplace.

Then a chance conversation with one of the researchers revealed that she too was looking for health after a breakdown, although her recovery was going better than mine. Also a former journalist, she had developed fatigue while working at a newspaper. Conflicted and compromised by some of her assignments, she had forced herself to work through it, even though her body was telling her to stop. Recovery, for her, meant taking a year off to learn how to go more slowly and authentically, gradually pacing herself back into life. Bedridden at first, she had gently progressed to meeting friends for coffee once or twice a week, then to a few part-time projects (only those that made her heart sing), and finally back into office life (she was now working four days a week and cared deeply about the charity's mission).

On hearing all of this, part of me fixated on her diagnosis: ME. Of course – that's it! I must have chronic fatigue syndrome, too. After all, I'm always exhausted; my legs feel like lead; my head's scrambled. But another, deeper part of me recognised the patterns behind the label: the drive to succeed, the faking, the willingness to suppress symptoms and overcompensate by trying even harder. And, of course, I also now recognised the remedy: slow down, let go, stop trying to make it better with even harder graft. *Give up the fight.*

I was nearly ready. After three weeks in the new job, shunting myself through yet another day of saying one thing and feeling another, I knew I wouldn't go in the next morning. 'Yet another failure,' said the thoughts in my mind. But this time, I didn't spiral down into self-recrimination. I looked up 'chronic fatigue' on the web. Some of the symptoms fitted me; others didn't. But the treatment plan resonated:

- Don't try to make yourself better through willpower.
- Accept how you feel.
- Stop struggling but don't wallow – don't retreat to bed for ever.
- Slow, small steps – pace yourself.
- Expect to take as long to get better as you've already been ill.

Expect to take as long to get better as you've already been ill? I'd already been ill for *two and a half years*. Yet I thought, 'I can do that. Because I know I can't carry on like this any more.'

I broached the subject with my (new) therapist at our next session. 'I think I might have ME,' I said.

'In that case,' he replied, 'you'll probably be disabled for the rest of your life.'

His words hit home, but I didn't feel dispirited. I felt relieved. If that's true, I reflected, then it really is okay to let go, to do nothing. There may be nothing I can do to change the way I feel. Okay. I'm ready to let go.

This wasn't a weak surrender. I didn't return to bed, at least not in the same way as I had before. I started resting *on* the bed, lying down without mentally beating myself up, neither hiding under the duvet nor pressurising myself to get up and seek a new job or treatment. I stopped attending the support groups and instead went for short, gentle walks, maybe just to the bus stop and back. Every other day or so, I would arrange to meet someone for tea. I had started to connect with a few people at the meditation centre and our discussions were light and optimistic, rather than focused on depression or addiction, as tended to happen at the support group sessions. I stopped looking for work and applied for sickness benefit, accepting that now was not the time for a new career. I stopped searching for new information and support, and I mostly stopped reading books, except for a few pages at a time (as recommended in the guides to pacing). I stopped ringing the Samaritans to tell them how awful I felt, and started telling myself that it was okay to be me, just as I was.

And I meditated. My day became infused with the approach to life I had learned over the previous few months. The literature on chronic fatigue explained that it was exhausting to think or talk constantly, and that conversations, reading and activities that required intense concentration or induced stress should be carefully rationed. Meditation practice, I realised, had already shown me a way of managing this. Instead of rushing to do or think, I just let myself watch my breath and feel my body as I moved slowly, gently, through each moment. Although I still felt the symptoms of depression – dissociation, restlessness, body tension, negative thoughts – I didn't sink into rumination or despondency, as I knew the stress of that would sap even more energy. Crucially, I now had an alternative – I followed my breath as my emotions swung back and forth. For the first time, outside of my formal meditation practice, I allowed myself to live slowly and deliberately, offering kindness to myself and my predicament, without expecting anything in return.

Around ten days into this experiment – on a Friday morning in late August – I was lying in the bath. Suddenly I noticed something odd. I was relaxed. My bones weren't aching. My muscles weren't tense. My heart wasn't racing. My thoughts weren't on a loop of impending disaster. I felt *okay*!

It had been thirty-five months since I'd experienced anything like this. 'Oh my God,' I whispered to myself, 'I remember this.' Gingerly, I stepped out of the bath and got dressed, very slowly, unable quite to believe what was happening. I *still* felt okay. I decided to go out for a walk. Stepping outside my flat, onto the pavement, I looked up. It was a beautiful late summer's day. The sun was shining, and I could feel its warmth on my face. It was wonderful, even though I still felt physically fragile. 'Wow,' I said to myself, mouthing the word silently, 'this is amazing.' I turned around, shuffled back inside, and burst into floods of tears. But these were tears of relief, joy and sadness – all mixed together – rather than of rage. As I wept and wept, falling to the floor, letting out great sobbing, heaving wails, I thought the crying might never stop. A chink had appeared in the chain mail of depression.

Practice to try: Mindful tea-drinking

If you are feeling very depressed or anxious, even short periods of meditation can seem overwhelming at first. So bringing mindfulness to everyday activities such as drinking a cup of tea, cleaning your teeth or going for a walk is a gentle way to begin. It's also a helpful way to develop your practice. Below are a few suggestions on how to practise mindful tea-drinking. Obviously, you can make and drink the tea in any way you like, or you can replace it with another regular activity. The important thing is to let go into seeing, feeling, tasting, touching and hearing, and to return gently to the senses whenever you notice the mind straying into thought.

1. Pay attention to the sound of the water heating and boiling in the kettle. Hear its bubbling and gurgling. Can you see wisps of steam coming from the spout? Does the kettle subtly shake from the movement of the water inside? Be open to your senses, rather than try to analyse what's happening.

2. Notice the feeling of being in your environment: your bottom's contact with the chair or the floor, if you're sitting down; the weight of your feet on the ground, if you're standing.

3. Pouring the tea, watch the colour of the water change as it meets the teabag. Be interested in the transformation from clear water to tea, and the tinkling of liquid as it fills the cup. When your mind wanders into thought, as it probably will, gently return your attention to sensing.

4. Lifting the teabag out with a spoon, feel the touch of the handle against your fingers, and the weight of the bag dropping away as you tip it into the bin. Let yourself hear any related sounds, such as the opening and closing of the bin lid. Notice any tendency to do this on autopilot, and come back to present-moment sensing when you find you've drifted to distraction.

5. If you take milk and sugar, be interested in how you feel as you reach for and add these ingredients to the brew. Do you really want them? How do you know?

6. Notice the warming of the cup that contains the hot liquid. How do your hands feel as you hold it?

7. Now, bring the cup to your lips. Be interested in how your hand and arm know how to move in this direction without you having to tell them consciously what to do.

8. Take a sip of tea. Rather than gulping it down, see if you can let the taste tickle your tongue. Perhaps gently move the liquid around your mouth. Savour the taste – is it pleasant? Or perhaps you'de prefer it stronger or weaker? You don't have to do anything about it (unless you choose to). Just be aware of your sensations and the liking or disliking of them. If there are thoughts, let them enter into and then pass through your mind without following them. Try to stay with the tasting. Notice without judgement any desire to rush the drinking, and any impatience that comes.

9. When you decide to swallow the tea, notice how that decision is made. Is it a conscious choice, or does it happen automatically? Stay present to the swallowing, the reflex movements in the back of the mouth and the throat, the

trickle of liquid down into the stomach. How does it feel to be swallowing?

10. Notice how the liquid seems to disappear. Is there a point when the tea stops being separate from you? When and how do you recognise that moment?

11. Pause now, noticing any feelings of irritation, or thoughts such as: Hurry up, I've got better things to do. Or perhaps a sense of peace or stillness enters you. If so, where do you feel it? Is it changing from moment to moment, or staying the same? Maybe there's something else going on in your mind and body, perhaps unrelated to the tea-drinking, pulling you into thoughts of the past or the future. If so, just notice it. Whatever comes up in your experience is okay from the perspective of meditation – there's no right or wrong thing to notice. Bring gentle awareness to whatever emerges. Becoming conscious of how much the mind wanders is a sign of growing awareness.

12. Take a look around you, opening your eyes to your surroundings without buying into evaluations about them. Just be aware of any thoughts or feelings that come up.

13. Now, return your attention to the cup of tea in your hand. (Has the temperature dropped?) Watch as you decide when to begin the process of taking another sip. Return to step seven, and continue drinking the tea until the cup is empty, or you decide to stop drinking. If the latter, be curious about what is prompting that decision. Has the tea gone cold, has the taste changed, is there an impulse to get on with your next activity? (If the latter, what does that feel like? Is there a place in your body where you feel it most strongly?) Whatever

you choose to do in each moment, try to watch the experience from an engaged observer's perspective.

You don't have to follow these steps like a strict to-do list. The key is to open yourself to the spirit of the practice, sensing with gentle precision what's happening, moment by moment, and coming back to sensing whenever you notice you've drifted into thought.

Why mindful tea-drinking?

Bringing mindfulness to simple activities like drinking tea trains us to direct attention consciously. We might think we choose what we're paying attention to in life, but in reality most of us are driven by habit and impulse. By deliberately choosing to attend to an activity, we slow things down and let ourselves become aware of the process of attending and perhaps how little control we usually have over it. We might notice the repeated wandering of the mind as we attempt to stay with what's happening right now.

We are learning to see what's often obscured by distraction. By coming back repeatedly to the various aspects of tea-drinking, we are cultivating the capacity to focus. And because we're practising this with gentleness, without judging ourselves or striving to reach some goal (even the goal of becoming better at paying attention), we are simultaneously training in acceptance and compassion.

Mindfulness means paying attention with the senses, in the body – feeling, touching, seeing, hearing and tasting. Sensing always happens within the body and in the present moment (you can't feel something in your thoughts, or in the past or future), so this tuning in to sensing helps to bring us into the reality of here and now. Sensing mindfully thus creates a space where we can experience what *is happening*, rather than indentifying with thinking about what should happen or what has already happened. It's a chance to practise resting the analytical mind that habitually searches for solutions, even when none is available.

We are also practising conscious choice. By watching how we make simple decisions – pouring water, disposing of a teabag, swallowing – we are bringing a deliberate awareness to activities that are often performed half-asleep. (Have you ever found yourself putting milk in a friend's preferred black tea just because that's how you take it yourself?) If we are unaware of how we get caught up, it's impossible to become free. But if we can start to practise seeing when we are acting on autopilot, through force of habit, or on impulse, we have already created the possibility of something different. We are starting to know what we are doing as we are doing it. This knowledge can begin with tea-drinking, and can then expand to every aspect of life.

CHAPTER TWO

Crossing the Abyss

What can we gain by sailing to the moon
if we are not able to cross the abyss that
separates us from ourselves?

Thomas Merton[1]

In the first few months of emerging from depression, I was buoyed by euphoria. I'd been used to living in sluggishness and tension. Now, suddenly, I felt energised and free. With the constant churn of obsession and self-criticism abating, the basic tasks of living, for so long a struggle, once again seemed manageable. It was like someone had flicked a switch in me, lifting the curse that had cast a dark veil over my life.

My practical circumstances weren't much different, but my approach to them transformed. I found the confidence to make calls to editors, and job offers poured in. My flat – so long a prison – now felt like a place of sanctuary. London was a vibrant city of endless possibilities rather than a vast pit of noisy, unwelcoming strangers. All the happy perspectives denied me in the depths of depression returned with interest. Fresh from what had felt like hell, I experienced a wellspring of joy.

This remarkable shift occurred over just a couple of weeks – those initial moments of magic in the bath extending at first for a few hours, then over a full day, then for several days in a row. There was an occasional snap back to anxiety and rumination, but I was so thrilled by the glimpses of light that even when the symptoms of depression returned for a while, I didn't feel depressed. I slowed down and watched my mind, trusting that the upward trend would continue. And it did. After a fortnight, there were no more relapses.

I continued with daily meditation. It seemed clear to me that remission was connected with the practice. A sense of anchoring grew within me – whatever thoughts or sensations came up during a meditation session, I practised the same way, letting them be present in awareness and continuing to follow the breath. In, out, in, out, observing and feeling the texture of breathing, a moment-by-moment experience of air entering, filling and leaving the body. And when I noticed my mind had wandered, usually into abstract thought, I would gently return to breath sensations.

Repeating this process again and again, it seemed I was strengthening steadiness and presence, less at the mercy of every whim. There was less attachment, too. Instead of being facile words with which I felt taunted, the phrase 'letting go' started to gain some practical meaning. I began to see how it could be practised.

It became easier to see the patterns that pulled on me, and with that came the possibility of unhooking from them. Instead of being dragged around by thoughts and impulses, I was more able to notice them arising in the mind, beckoning for attention and action. I began to experiment with *not* following their call. I found the fact that this was possible interesting and empowering.

Freed from depression, I discovered I could feel again. As a child, I had sensed things acutely, but then I'd felt frozen for such a long time. Now, I was once more in touch with my emotions. I felt sad more often – grieving for the recent lost years – but also unprecedented contentment and peace. Meditation invited a dropping of my psychic armoury, putting me in contact with life through the senses, rather than filtered by abstractions of thought. And from the perspective of an expansive awareness, trained through the practice of mindfulness, joy and sadness could be equally exquisite. I was sensitive to pain, it was true, but I no longer felt depressed by it. The sensations weren't smothered by a cloak of suppression, or avoided by constant running.

As well as reconnecting with my interior self, I started making new friends. In the months before the depression lifted, I had started to visit the Buddhist centre more often – for further instruction, but also for support and fellowship. There were regular open practice sessions, and a group usually went to the pub afterwards. I soon felt comfortable in this crowd. Some had been practising for more than twenty years, and these experienced meditators exuded gentleness, strength and warmth. From the stories they told, meditation was clearly key to their demeanour. There was no room for sanctimony or posturing. They exhibited a genuine and earthy recognition of the ups and downs of living, and a willingness to experience, work with and, where possible, enjoy them. I was powerfully drawn to their openness of spirit.

Intrigued and inspired, I began to deepen my connection to Buddhism. I attended weekend meditation programmes, centring on the practice of mindfulness of breathing. The Sanskrit term for this is *shamatha*, which translates as 'calm abiding'. Calmly abiding with whatever arises, we gain insight into patterns of mind and experience. Rather than being drawn automatically into our usual patterns of thinking and reacting, we notice them with interest, becoming ever more familiar with their pull. On these weekends, a group of twenty or thirty of us would practise mindfulness of breathing for seven or eight hours a day.

Studying in parallel with practice, I learned more about Buddhists' central observations. Having understood that life is stressful because we keep trying to cling to changing events, we realise freedom when we acknowledge that everything experienced is in flux. This includes what we usually call 'ourselves'. When we look carefully, we find there is nothing that corresponds with what we tend to construe as 'me' – a single, separate, fixed entity from which we live out life. We are more a set of ever-changing 'heaps' (*skandhas* in Sanskrit). These comprise physical processes, sensory events, perceptions of those events, inclinations of mind and body such as thoughts, emotions and reactions, as well as the consciousness that experiences all of this happening. Despite how it might seem, no single entity is running the show.

The philosopher David Hume had a similar insight:

When I enter most intimately into what I call myself, I always stumble on some particular perception or other, of heat or cold, light or shade, love or hatred, pain or pleasure. I can never catch myself at any time without a perception, and never can observe anything but the perception ... I may venture to affirm of the rest of mankind, that they are nothing but a bundle of different perceptions, which succeed each other with an inconceivable rapidity, and are in perpetual flux and movement.[2]

Meditation could be described as a way of 'entering intimately' into experience, and it can reveal for us the truth in Hume's observations. In the practice we notice all the heaps, changing moment by moment in conscious awareness. Once we can see how experience arises, we may work with it skilfully, rather than from unconscious habit. Through practising mindfulness, we become more aware of what's happening as it's happening, and can begin to step out of the cycle of what is known in Buddhism as 'dependent origination': the otherwise incessant flow of events, and automatic reactions to those events that tend to drive us through life.

For me, it was hugely heartening to observe these patterns when so much in my mind, body and life before had seemed like an unholy jumble. And it felt even better to know I was on a path that would lead further into this exploration of life, complete with directions, signposts and support structures.

It seems obvious, when you look carefully, that everything in life is experienced in the mind. Therefore, in order to live well, the most effective method is not so much tinkering with external circumstances but learning to work skilfully with experience. As the Buddha put it: 'No one can harm you, not even your worst enemy, as much as your own mind untrained ... and no one can help you, not even your most loving mother and father, as much as your own mind well trained.'[3] Training the mind – which includes working with experience in the body too – is the key to well-being.

Finally, here was a way that made sense. Why had it taken me so long to find it?

I clearly remember my first encounter with Buddhism. I was twelve years old when I picked up a book on world religions in the school library. I read about the four noble truths and a few other core Buddhist observations, and was immediately struck by their relevance. I also read descriptions of the Buddhist way of life, which seemed to involve a lot of restraint, definitely no intoxication, and the supposed end goal of nirvana, which the book described as 'a total cessation of existence'. This didn't sound like a whole lot of fun at the time: a life of heavy restriction along the way to ultimate extinction. 'Hmm,' I mused, 'maybe I'll come back to that later.'

A decade later, when suffering was already gnawing at my insides, I had buried any sense of metaphysical interest and instead was distracting – or white-knuckling – my way through a series of break-ups and breakdowns. During the early days of my long depression, I remember grimly marching up and down Clapham High Street, muscles rigid with tension and fear, muttering with menace at my own reviled emotions: 'I'm gonna fight, and I'm gonna win.' When this didn't work, I was lost. There were so many supposed solutions to the problem of human misery, yet human misery was everywhere. I was confused, in my lowest and most vulnerable state, and in no position to make valid judgements about treatment.

So I just tended to go with whatever was offered. The doctor gave me antidepressants, so I took them. He seemed half-hearted about the chances of success, so I was hardly imbued with confidence, especially as I'd never had much faith in pills. To reduce existential angst to equalising chemical imbalances and targeting faulty neurotransmitters seemed both alien and alienating to me. Although my depression felt awful, it never seemed devoid of meaning. I was convinced that my symptoms were telling me something – they weren't just random violence. Even at my worst moments, this belief helped me cope with suicidal thoughts. I felt as if I had been set a task – to understand and learn from what was happening.

This wasn't merely a matter of physiology but also of experience. Taking pills didn't speak to my sense of woundedness; it felt more like a sticking plaster. And, as with all treatments, it helps to connect with the narrative that accompanies it. Studies show a strong placebo response to antidepressants[4] – their effect is significantly enhanced if the patient believes in their efficacy. But I never thought they would work for me, so it was hardly surprising that the results were disappointing. Over the years I took Prozac, Seroxat, Venlafaxine, Citalopram and a number of other antidepressants, but I never noticed any correlation between mood and medicine. There were *effects*, for sure – sexual dysfunction, drowsiness and (in the case of Seroxat and Effexor) an unpleasant sensation of water on the brain – but I experienced neither relief nor the flattening of emotion that many people describe.

Some people who experience depression find Western medicine's approach a comfort, as it frees them from the stigma that many of us impose on ourselves ('Oh, it's just my faulty neurotransmitters'). But while it certainly wasn't useful to think that my depression was 'all my own fault', nor that I should be able to beat it with willpower alone, a purely biological interpretation didn't seem to help, either. If depression were due to physiology alone, then I really was stuck, with nowhere else to turn once I acknowledged that the medicine wasn't working for me. I felt helpless and desperate, yet this interpretation of my condition seemed to suggest that I should just resign myself to a lifetime of misery. I found that prospect profoundly disempowering, and disempowerment itself is a risk factor and symptom of depression. When I took on the label 'depressive' it confirmed and reinforced the experience of depression, which in turn confirmed and reinforced the label. I tended to seek refuge in psychiatric diagnoses of mental illness during my darkest hours, when I suffered rock-bottom confidence and felt the greatest need for certainty. But identifying as mentally ill never guided me out of unhappiness; instead, it just increased my sense of self-imposed stigma and incapacity – further filling the padding on my cell walls.

I found similar difficulties in the various twelve-step groups I attended. These fellowships are modelled on the original Alcoholics Anonymous programme, developed in the United States in the 1930s. I came to them via a suggestion from my first therapist, who pointed me in the direction of some books on co-dependency. In these I discovered the existence of a network of people who had the habit of losing themselves in relationships.

Every twelve-step programme begins when the addict admits powerlessness over whatever it is they're addicted to – drink, drugs, sex, gambling, romantic relationships – and hands their life over to the care of a higher power (the word 'God' tends to be used, but everyone is free to interpret this in their own way). The remaining eleven steps are a guide through the process of looking at and letting go of the past – making and sharing a 'moral inventory' of your life, admitting 'wrongs', and asking God to remove 'defects' – that lead to a commitment to a regime of prayer, meditation and helping other sufferers as a means to ongoing recovery.

I found some aspects of these twelve-step programmes helpful. Wherever I was, no matter how lonely I was feeling, I could usually find a meeting of supportive strangers. There was space to talk and listen, and a shared sense of suffering and hope. The principles of 'taking the steps' – recognising your limitations; looking at and letting go of unhelpful, compulsive behaviour; starting to act from a sense of awareness, gratitude and altruism – is a sensible way to free yourself from self-destructive habits. But after two years, and hundreds of meetings, my depression was as entrenched as ever.

My understanding of certain elements in these programmes seemed to exacerbate low mood in me. I found the emphasis on powerlessness difficult. The more I was reminded of it, the more the thought loomed large in my mind – 'I ... am ... powerless ...' I even felt powerless for not being able to admit my powerlessness properly (it's supposed to be a way of letting go). I seemed unable to give my will to a higher power, which contributed to the belief that my defects must be insurmountable. Within the framework of the twelve-step programmes, I judged what I saw as my failings harshly, giving further fuel to my self-critical patterns of thinking.

For me, it also didn't help that we were encouraged to call ourselves 'co-dependents' or 'addicts' each time we began to speak in front of the group (in the same way as AA members are encouraged to label themselves 'alcoholics'). While this is meant to break down denial, repeated identification with the problem seemed to keep me stuck *within* that problem, making it seem ever more permanent, a core identity. It became yet another label with which I could attack myself.

An atmosphere of gloom seemed to pervade many meetings.

Perhaps not having reached the stage of being able to help others, many of us were looking for support and salvation through sharing and offloading our burdens of unhappiness. But this rarely made for an easy meeting, and I didn't often feel better by the end. Unable to cope with my own suffering, I was dragged further down by the pain of others. Already stuck in negative thoughts, it probably didn't help to tell my story of depression over and over again, reinforcing out loud the stressful narrative I was caught up in. The idea of recovery was good, but I couldn't connect to an embodiment of it.

So the drugs and support groups both failed to lift me out of depression, and the same could be said of the approach on which I pinned most of my hopes during those long, bleak years: psychotherapy. This, too, had its uses, providing a mirror that enabled me to see how I made life difficult, and offering a source of support, solace and direction. However, given my tendency to seek solutions from others (that co-dependency again), I viewed the therapists as ultimate sources of wisdom, throwing myself at them time and again. I hoped that their unconditional positive regard would somehow rub off on me. I did become accustomed – perhaps for the first time – to an intimate warmth in an adult relationship, but the nature of that relationship, with projected power always resting in the therapist, meant I still didn't learn how to give that warmth to myself, or carry it with me outside the consulting room. The good stuff invariably came from someone else, which still left me in the same old dependent place.

Meditation and Buddhism offered something different. While dropping habitual behaviour was central to both the twelve-step programmes and the therapy, the Buddhist approach to it was kind, clear and empowering. In mindfulness meditation there was a practical means to bring patterns to consciousness, and to work with them skilfully.

This means is evident in one of the Buddha's discourses, *The Four Foundations of Mindfulness*. In this teaching, the student receives guidance on how to pay attention when meditating. The practice begins with mindfulness of breathing, and continues with bringing awareness to the body, feelings, mental events and finally the wider world. This simple system of observing and working with the phenomena of experience opened a window on my world that brought deeper insights, and more moments of contentment, than all of my forays into Western treatment combined.

Because habitual patterns are seen as temporary obfuscations – born of a confused mind rather than any basic deficiency – the path can be gentle. We are not defective, and we don't need a higher power to release us. It's more a case of realising an existing wisdom, using tools we already possess. We discover an awareness that already resides within us. Practice, therefore, becomes not so much something to achieve, but something to drop into – we need only become willing to allow wise ways of being we already know in our minds and feel in our hearts.

With this in mind, my experience of emerging from depression made sense. A lifetime of defending against difficulties and clinging to pleasure had led only to despair, which I had attempted to treat with the same old prescription – struggling to fight, withdraw from or think through problems, and desperately seeking solutions from external sources. Until I started meditating, nothing had touched the deeply ingrained belief that there was something wrong that I needed to make good, something outside that I had to grasp. So my struggle continued. Meditation enabled a transformation in my view and my experience, as 'letting go of fighting' moved from idea to reality. As I dropped all attempts to think, fight or run to recovery, I discovered a present-centred connection to experience. Instead of the stress of grasping and avoidance – most of which was propelled by my own thoughts – I found some relaxation. As I let go, the depression dissolved. This wasn't just a story, not just a thought. *I felt the relief in my flesh and bones.*

Still, the psychic peace was fragile. One old friend, observing my new interests, said: 'Well, Ed, you certainly win the award for the biggest life U-turn.' And plenty of forces were pulling on old strings. I was still freelancing for lifestyle magazines, as well as promoting a luxury car brand. However, the more comfortable I felt in meditation centres, the less I felt at home in media offices. And although I was sensitised by my practice, I wasn't yet greatly strengthened by it. I remained ill-equipped to manage the open conflict between the prevailing attitudes of the world I worked in and the path I knew I had to follow. Mostly, I protected myself by working from home, but around nine months after my remission had begun I was embedded within teams where the exposure was too great. Whereas previously I'd been unaware of the influence of environment on my experience, this time I felt and witnessed the tension rising as I frazzled in the frantic atmosphere.

I slipped back into depression, and my bodily sensations turned unpleasant again, so I retreated back into my head, once again desperately trying to find solutions by thinking. But the thoughts that came were just as stressful as ever: 'Oh, no! I'm right back where I started. Perhaps meditation doesn't help after all. I've been fooling myself. I still can't cope. Why can't I survive in the workplace like most people? Buddhism won't pay my bills. Who am I kidding? Why can't I sort myself out?' The old racing mind fuelled the old panic – pumping heart, clenched muscles, churning gut, chronic restlessness. In turn, this led to more thoughts: 'I can't do another three years of this ...'

But this time it wasn't *quite* the same as before. While the fear was still intense, especially when I decided to resign again ('They'll never take me back after *this!*'), I drew on the memory that remission was possible, and on the framework that let it occur. There was still a demanding, expectant quality in the way I met my experience – 'If I meditate, this should go away again, right? Well, I'm meditating, so why isn't it going away yet?' – but at least I had *some* sense of what to do. I also recognised that I had relapsed partly due to the stress of forcing myself into roles that no longer fitted my values. I knew that if I wanted to be well, I needed to live a more integrated life.

Whereas depression had once seemed like an iron blanket over everything, this time I noticed small gaps in the pain – moments, sometimes extending into hours – when its tight grip loosened. And even when its hold was strong, the experience wasn't monotonous. Although the sensations were mostly unpleasant, at least they were constantly changing: sometimes stomach cramps or throbbing temples dominated; at other times I was pulled into my head, consumed with thoughts about what had gone wrong and how I might solve it. Sometimes I felt agitated and anxious; at other times simply overcome with fatigue. Rather than enduring a single, static experience, I could perceive that depression consisted of constellations of thoughts, emotions and sensations, shifting from moment to moment. There were patterns and tendencies for sure. But this was not an unchanging, rigid experience. As I described the events of my psyche, one of my meditation instructors explained, 'Ed, you see. It's not solid.'

The phrase resonated. *Not solid.* Therefore, it was not permanent. Indeed, it was already in transition. Perhaps everything had always been moving, but now I was more aware of it. Perhaps part of what had kept me stuck was the *idea* that I was stuck, an idea reinforced by the labels I had grasped – for explanation, ease and certainty. The meditation training had allowed me to perceive things differently – I noticed sensory experience, felt in the body, without being so caught up in my thoughts about it. When thoughts came, I was able to notice these too, without always believing what they told me. And I saw how both thoughts and feelings were changing, moment by moment, which helped me to see that they didn't have the power I had previously given them.

I also felt support from the Buddhist community. My new friends didn't desert me, but they also didn't feed my crisis by always talking about it or attempting to sort me out. Generous with their time, they were willing just to be with me, even though I can't have been much fun. I felt the benefit of their practical compassion.

After three months on the relapse rollercoaster, my mood lightened – quite suddenly, just as it had before. I was offered some work at the Mental Health Foundation, and this helped heal my work–life split. At last I was working with colleagues in the service of wellbeing. Soon I was offered a longer-term, paid contract, writing and researching a report on the benefits of physical exercise for depression. As well as continuing my daily meditation practice, group practice at least once a week and weekend intensive courses every couple of months, I began attending longer retreats, making several visits to the Dechen Choling centre in central France.

The centre runs programmes throughout the year, offering space, facilities and support for people looking to deepen their meditation practice, away from the distractions of their home environments. My visits were powerful. Not only could I dedicate myself to my practice for longer, but it was inspiring to join a community that was run on Buddhist principles. Here were people who had chosen to spend weeks, months or sometimes years living and working in a contemplative space.

Although I was taking steps to orient my life in ways that were more authentic and congruent, I started to feel quite estranged from the mainstream world. There seemed few places now where I could share my experiences, where I felt understood. Even though I could talk openly about the mind at the Mental Health Foundation, there were no fellow meditators. My family and old friends were pleased I had finally found something that was help-ing, but I couldn't find the words to describe the changes that were happening within me. I was dropping away from the twelve-step fellowships, and my current therapist, though supportive, had no experience with Buddhism.

Meditation is such an intimate experience. Its insights – espe-cially when described by others – tend to be opaque until you give yourself to it. While it is possible to describe what happens when you practise, the words only ever hint at the full experience. They cannot do it justice, because meditation opens us to a non-conceptual, sensory world that is, by nature, ineffable. Without the experience as a reference point, non-practitioners can find descriptions of meditation strange or even nonsensical. So, while meditation was revelatory and satisfying for me, I was in what Pema Chödrön calls 'the in-between space': my practice was still new and at odds with the way of life that had previously sustained me, albeit in a dysfunctional way. The foundations of something different were being laid, but the ground was shaky. I felt vulner-able, because I had decided to leave behind the safety of a world I had known for decades.

In the summer of 2005, the ground shook once more. My con-tract with the Mental Health Foundation had come to an end, and I wasn't sure what to do next. I had learned a lot about conventional approaches to well-being, including the importance of research in testing and communicating the value of treatments, but there seemed to be something missing in the mainstream mental health arena. My own experience told me that the principles and practices of Buddhism go right to the root of stress and suffering. They also show us how to see and start to unhook from the processes that sustain it in the mind, body and wider world. These practices didn't promise a quick solution, but they had already taught me to look at the mind in a radically different way.

From what I saw, meditation might occasionally receive a mention in the mental health literature, usually in discussions on spirituality or alternative medicine, but this was rare. When I considered the enormous benefits I was reaping from observing and working with my mind in this way, it seemed curious – and disappointing – that the approach was largely ignored in mainstream mental health settings.

As I drifted without purpose, my old symptoms began to return. This time, though, there was no sudden falling through a trapdoor; rather, I experienced a gradual evaporation of confidence and energy. I began to feel lethargic and listless, especially on my cycle ride to work, as if I were pedalling towards barriers that I'd rather not face. As the days of low mood began to outnumber the 'good' days, I began to feel frightened of succumbing to the darkness once more. When anxious thinking itself darkens one's mood, the thought 'Oh no, here we go again!' can easily become a self-fulfilling prophecy, even when relatively mild symptoms of depression arise. In the face of the conflicts rising within me, I began to drown again. Although my commitment to a contemplative path was clear, my practice was still far from mature, especially considering my starting point. This time it may have slowed the descent, but when faced with challenging circumstances, I still couldn't draw on the resources to cope. In my head I started running from the fear again, but that merely led me further into the pit.

Around this time, I was due to attend a month-long retreat. It was meant to be a chance to deepen my practice, and it would be pretty intense: meditating for around twelve hours each day, including eating in silence. Consumed with anxiety more often than not, I was tempted to cancel, but several experienced practitioners advised me to go.

The retreat proved to be a revelation, although not a particularly comfortable one. For the first few days, sitting with a group of around forty other meditators in a tent in the woods, I struggled to let go of my thoughts: 'Go home! You'll never manage a month of this. Maybe you should move to Colorado. Why does everyone else look so calm? You're crazy, you know, mentally ill. I mean, look at your mood swings. You're so bipolar, meditation can't help you. You need medication – lithium or something.' Every once in a while I was able to feel my breath while such thoughts continued to bark at me; most of the time I was caught up in the barking. My heart thumped with fear. I might have looked calm as I sat cross-legged on a cushion, but inside I was jelly. My teeth, neck, shoulders and legs all clenched, as if trying to stop the internal shaking.

Then, after about five days, tears came. They began during an interview with a meditation instructor, which were scheduled every few days. Although bunged up in my thoughts, the emotion within me was bursting at the seams. As I dropped my attention into my breath again and again, it was as if I was being softened up. It was getting ever more difficult to contain what I was feeling inside. I'm not sure what triggered the flow – it could have been a kind comment or a gentle touch on my hand – but the barriers suddenly collapsed and it all started pouring out. Wave after wave of sobs, surging from my body.

Before long, this started happening during the meditation itself. I'd be sitting in silence, then suddenly a great ocean of emotion would well up and the crying would begin. I'd leave the tent, sit under a nearby tree, and just let the waves happen, wailing without restraint, over and over. To my surprise, when the tears finally subsided, I felt a huge release. It was like an emptying out from within my body, as if the meditation had opened a valve. As the emotions were released, the pace of my thinking slowed.

In the space and stillness of the retreat, I was able to observe all this happening – the upsurging and outpouring of energy – unhindered by everyday concerns. I was aware of body sensations that I had never noticed before: a tingling in my nose before each episode, building into pressure, like fingers pushing outwards from inside my face; and a tendency to yawn, as if air were being forced from my mouth. I watched the speed of my thoughts continue to slow, and increasingly felt a sense of mental and physical space.

At times, between the bouts of crying, there was a calm I'd never known before. My body felt warm, soft, unburdened, light. Looking at my fellow practitioners during the (silent) meals, or at the cows that grazed in the surrounding fields, or at the luminous sky and the clouds that crossed it, or at the ants scurrying in lines across the pathways, I saw the world afresh. There was a new vividness to colours, a new depth to textures, a new sharpness to lines – the environment became a kaleidoscopic feast for the senses. It was wonderful, like receiving all the riches of the world at once. It was bliss to watch a grasshopper landing on a blade of grass, wash itself, and hop away. I felt attuned, connected, more a part of life than I ever had before. I felt in touch with myself as a mind and a body, and in touch with the world around me. Sharing this with a senior student, I was struck when he told me, without any arrogance: 'It's like that for me most of the time.'

Others on the retreat were changing, too. There was a palpable shift in atmosphere as the days went by and the attendees seemed to become gentler and kinder. The boundaries between us dissolved, and there was a growing sense of mutual acceptance, communion, even love. Some were going through turbulence like my own, and this was accepted as part of the process – we were neither rejected nor turned into projects to fix. There was trust and understanding that everyone was getting what they needed, just by allowing the space to stop, to unfold, to be.

These retreats are rarely a picnic for anyone. Some of the attendees' hearts ache; for others, the agony is in their bones. Sensitised by intensive practice, the pain can increase at first, while surges of anger or sadness can strike in the body like bolts of electricity. Moreover, there are core realities to consider. At one point, an instructor silently held up a card for us to contemplate. It read: 'IMPERMANENCE'. This was a signal to meditate on the inevitability of one's own passing. 'Death is real, and comes without warning,' we were reminded. 'This body will be a corpse.' As the sign was raised, I turned to a new friend sitting beside me. After a moment of connection, we both collapsed in laughter. Was this really how we'd chosen to spend our summer?

It seemed absurd. But, of course, it's anything but. Death *is* real and it (often) comes without warning. This body *will* be a corpse. Somehow, by turning our hearts to this fact, in the deeply supportive environment of the retreat, the result wasn't depression but relief – from having to spend the whole time shielding ourselves from the truth through frenetic activity or worry. By recognising and accepting the world on its terms, we were able to receive its marvels in exchange.

The waves in my mind and body continued. During the second and third weeks of the retreat, the outpouring of tears came four or five times every day, usually preceded by an intense restlessness and an increase in the speed and frequency of thinking. The thoughts involuntarily turned to the past and I grieved for long-gone events, feeling their pain deep within my body. Family crises, childhood loneliness, romantic rejections and life led in the mistaken belief that status and material possessions would bring peace – all of these appeared in my mind as rolling currents of sadness emanated from my chest and belly. It all passed through and out with the tears.

As the days wore on, I was more able to witness these scenes as an interested, caring observer. I was learning to hold my own hand through the storms. The retreat staff showed me how to do this by their own kind approach – they gave me time, space and a kindly presence when I needed it, often sitting with me as I cried.

The structure of the retreat – practice from dawn to dusk, mindful meals and walks, occasional group meetings to reflect on experience, time and space to exercise, rest and laugh – allowed mind and body patterns to be identified and released. Activity and distractions were minimised – reading was discouraged (too much thinking, too many words), as was contacting friends and family. The idea was just to be present, practise meditation, allow what happened to happen, and watch and experience it, with as much awareness and kindness as possible. There were no complicated techniques, no secret formulas. In fact, we hardly did anything at all – just letting go into being human.

Gradually, during the third and fourth weeks, the crying started to subside. The waves would come four, then three, then two times a day. In between, I felt happier and more relaxed than I'd ever been.

Then it was time to go home.

A warning was issued at the end of the retreat – re-entering the outside world can be difficult, we were told. The support structures created are suddenly absent, along with the smiling, friendly, opened-up friends with whom you have just shared an intimate and unusual experience. In their place, worldly concerns start calling for attention again – family and colleagues are awaiting your return, perhaps wondering what self-indulgence you've enjoyed while they've been taking care of business. Most people expect you to be pretty much the same as when you left them, and ready to take up the reins of life.

After a month of opening up to silence and space, you suddenly face traffic, news reports and a pile of unpaid bills, and the contrast can be stark. While retreats can be life-transforming, it can take time for the experience to integrate, and it's completely normal (although disappointing) for the magic, wonder and peace to ebb away, along with the experience of clarity and insight. This is just more impermanence with which to flow, but after a taste of life in Technicolor, the return to the monochrome world can be deflating.

It's generally advisable not to make any big changes when returning home from a retreat. There's a risk of being caught in a meditation buzz, infused with the belief that all of life can be like this now. This can lead to some unwise actions, such as leaving a long-term partner or quitting a stable job. I completely ignored this sound advice. Returning to a world that seemed grey and harsh, I was desperate to stay connected to the bright, new world I'd found in France. Although I was more settled, the waves of grief were still rolling, and it was most inconvenient to feel them when standing on a crowded bus or during a meeting with colleagues. When this happened, I wasn't sure what to do. Should I make my excuses and go to the bathroom and cry? Or should I suppress that urge, which might run the risk of allowing it to develop into depression? The more I thought about what to do, the more I was caught up in my head again, and the more I felt my body tightening. I was losing touch with the gorgeous openness I'd only just discovered. The more I resisted this closing down, or tried to find a solution to rectify it, the more it intensified.

I tried to set up an early morning sitting group at the local meditation centre, but very few people had the time – or inclination – to attend. As autumn closed in, it started to feel cold and dark at dawn, and my energy was waning. The gloom I had been stuck in before the retreat was returning yet again, propelled by storm clouds of thoughts that circled around my mind, ordering me to take one course, then another.

Actually, my heart knew what it wanted. Dechen Choling was pulling me back strongly. The retreat had hastened an unravelling, not easily contained in the framework of life at home, especially in someone with my vulnerability. I needed more support and more structure to be able to comprehend, allow and integrate the experiences I was having. In my somewhat confused state, I quickly made a mess of some professional and personal relationships, and found myself in a position where I had no immediate employment prospects and no romantic ties. So, in mid-November 2005, I picked up the phone, called the head of personnel at Dechen Choling, and asked if they needed any help. And, if so, could I provide it?

Two months later, a week before my thirty-third birthday, I boarded another train to Limoges, this time with a one-way ticket.

Practice to try: Mindfulness of breathing

The Buddha's *Four Foundations of Mindfulness* begins with attending to breathing. Watching and feeling the breath anchors the mind, giving it something to stay with and return to. When we notice that the mind is no longer following the breath, we're invited to acknowledge this and return. The more we practise, the more it's possible to observe the patterns of drifting that happen through our lives. We notice how often we are *not* paying attention, and where the mind tends to go. We see our patterns of getting lost in thought, emotion or sensation. The beauty of this is that as soon as we've noticed we're not paying attention, we're already back in mindfulness again. Simply by *observing* distraction, we're no longer caught in it. In that moment of noticing, we have a choice over what to do. By training the mind to return repeatedly to presence, to an anchor such as the breath in the body, we gradually enable a stability to develop.

Note: It can be helpful to be guided through meditation practice, especially at first. I've recorded audio guides to many of the practices found in this book, which you can find at www.edhalliwell.com

1. Find a quiet place, and sit on either a chair or a cushion. If you choose a chair, it's best if it has a firm, flat seat, which will help you hold your back upright (although not stiffly), rather than slumping backwards or forwards. Let the soles of your feet meet the ground, and bring your hands on to your lap, with the palms facing down. If you sit on a cushion, you can be cross-legged. Let your body relax as much as you can, inviting a sense of openness and confidence.

2. Decide how long to practise for. Your session can be as short as five minutes, or much longer. You may find it useful to set an alarm to tell you when to stop, so you don't have to think about it.

3. Bring attention to the sensations of breathing in your body, perhaps in the belly or the chest. Be curious about the process of breathing right now – how does *this* breath feel? Allow yourself to let go of thinking about or analysing the breath. Just *feel* it, as it is. You don't need to manipulate your breathing. Don't try to make each breath longer or deeper; just let it happen as it's happening. Follow its rhythms gently with attention: in and out, in and out, rising and falling, staying present to the sensations that come.

4. As for everything else that comes up in your experience – thoughts, emotions, body sensations, sounds and so on – allow them to be as they are, without identifying with any of them. Don't try to stop them, or push them out of your consciousness, or pay attention to them. Just allow what's happening to happen, without interference, as you keep directing gentle attention to your breathing.

5. When you notice that your mind has wandered, as it likely will often, acknowledge that this has happened with

kindness. You might even congratulate yourself for noticing. Remember, as soon as you're *aware* of the wandering, you have a choice about what to do next. Where did the mind go? Was it lost in thought, distracted by a sound, or by a feeling in the body? Again, there's no need to analyse; just acknowledge. Now, bring your attention back to the breath, and continue to follow it, in and out, moment by moment, with friendly interest.

6. Continue with steps three to five until it's time to stop.

Why aren't we trying to make a success of meditation?

Most of us take up meditation because we want something from it. Maybe we've read about the supposed benefits, and we'd like some of them for ourselves. It's good to have a sense of intention – without it, we can easily lose our motivation, especially when nothing much seems to be happening, or when something we don't like is looming on the horizon.

However, striving for success usually gets in the way. As soon as we try to get something else, or be somewhere else, we move into desire or aversion, thinking about where we'd like to be, rather than accepting the reality of how and where we are. This creates trouble. We try to work out how to get calm, or get rid of negativity, or force insight to come. We start pushing for results. Peace can come with practice, but only when we stop trying to hold on to, avoid or resist the experience of what's already happening. Peace comes only if we practise it as the method. That means letting go of struggle, and making friends with reality.

This is why I love the reminder 'Abandon all hope of fruition', which comes from a set of mind-training instructions developed by Atisha, an eleventh-century Tibetan teacher. I find its message of seeming doom funny – the joke in meditation is that we get somewhere by not trying to get anywhere. It invites us to set no targets, and not to judge ourselves constantly against some invented measure from the past or the future. If you're seeking peace, it will come when you stop measuring everything, including meditation, against an abstract yardstick.

This letting go of judging our practice is precisely what's trained in mindfulness of breathing. It's wonderfully simple. Just notice and follow the breath as it's happening right now, let everything be as it is, and when you notice that the mind has wandered, gently come back to the breath. Just keep practising this, and let the results take care of themselves.

CHAPTER THREE

In Contact, and Inspired

It is quite possible that in contact with
Western science and inspired by the spirit
of history, the original teaching of Gautama
[Buddha], revived and purified, may yet play a
large part in the direction of human destiny.

H.G. Wells[1]

Reculer pour mieux sauter!
[Retreat before you leap!]

French proverb

L iving at a retreat centre for one year is said to be the equiva-
lent of five years' practice in the outside world. At a place like
Dechen Choling, mirrors for the mind are everywhere. There's the
regular schedule of formal meditation, every morning and evening,
bookending the day with a time for stillness. But the possibilities
for practice go way beyond this. In a Buddhist community, all
activities – from cooking, cleaning, eating and drinking to driving,
gardening, working on the computer and attending meetings – are
considered forms of meditation, opportunities for mindfulness.

Meditative pauses are built into each day – at the start and end of meetings, before and after meals. The environment is scattered with reminders to practise ('Whatever you meet unexpectedly, join with meditation'; 'Don't try to be the fastest'; 'Be grateful to everyone'), placed strategically to encourage reflection. A contemplative mindset is invoked by the very architecture of a place where beautifully tended meditation halls take centre stage. In contrast to the everyday world, where everything seems to happen at high speed, and distracting temptations are manifold, retreat centres are carefully constructed holding containers for the mind, designed to allow it to slow down, settle and see itself. There is a sense of space in the landscape of Dechen Choling – around the centrepiece building, a former château, fields and woodland pathways are waiting to be explored. During the summer, most of the guests and instructors sleep in tents, inviting a connection with the earth, the air and the circadian rhythms of nature.

Living in such an environment can have powerful effects. It often struck me during my time at Dechen Choling that immersion in this type of community was like receiving all the therapies I'd tried at home rolled into one. There's the sense of shared purpose in freeing yourself from habitual patterns – similar to what binds people together in twelve-step groups. There's the commitment to looking at one's own process and its relationship to the wider world, which echoes the dynamics of therapy. There's the focus on practice as skills training, which reminded me of cognitive-behavioural training, during which clients are given homework to report back on during the next session. There are also similarities with Gestalt (the emphasis on present-moment embodiment), non-violent communication (right speech), practical philosophy (asking 'What makes a good life?') and positive psychology (a rigorous testing of methods that are thought to cultivate well-being).

Yet, with Buddhism, each of these methods forms part of a coherent culture, developed over the course of two and a half millennia, as a way to relieve suffering. With its sophisticated practices to uncover awareness and compassion, Buddhism offers a complete system to cultivate contentment. While the methods of Western psychology seem discrete, partial, fragmented and some-times contradictory, Buddhist cultures, it seems to me, address *every* aspect of mind, body and environment in relational context. Whereas Freud was gloomy about the prospects for success – the most we could expect, he said, was to turn neurosis into standard unhappiness – the message of the Buddha is much more optimistic. True well-being can be found, and the methods to uncover it are available to us.

My practice matured at Dechen Choling. As well as a couple of hours in formal meditation each day, I undertook two more month-long retreats, and a number of shorter intensive courses. I devoted myself to studying and practising a Buddhist approach through these formal programmes and voracious reading, as well as listening to and learning from the more experienced resi-dents and visitors. As much as I was able, I let myself marinate in mindfulness.

I surrendered to the schedule of work, too – cooking, cleaning, driving people to and from the train station and airport, working in the office. For the first time in my life since early childhood, I allowed myself not to be in control. I did not force myself to analyse or achieve or prove anything. I had no goal to reach. My sole inten-tion was to be here and now, experiencing life without trying to get anywhere else. In my free time, I gave myself up to the space of the land – walking in the fields, watching the cattle graze, listening to the wind, or just sitting and being.

Much of the time this was bliss. Letting life happen, going with its flow, brought moments of intense pleasure that came simply with the willingness to have them. Joy seemed to come from open-ing to the world around me, which I discovered was beautiful and amazing in its very existence. A spring of creativity arose within me, too. One day, I was inspired to go and buy a guitar, and soon I was playing and singing again. Until university days, I had always performed – both music and theatre – but the crowding of my life with material pursuits had drowned out any artistic calling. In the space of Dechen Choling, my love of music returned. I had a similar renaissance with languages, improving my French and Spanish, which I'd previously picked up during a gap year abroad. I realised that I thrived in community – the warmth of friendship after years of living alone was like sunlight to a flower.

There were difficulties as well. The intense sensations that had visited me the previous year frequently bubbled up, appearing first as that familiar pressure behind the nose, then gut churn-ing, heart pumping and sometimes an almost irresistible desire to run or scream. Alongside the extrovert that loved to be with others, I noticed that I often withdrew into solitude, closing myself off, even though this left me feeling contracted and lonely. I was deeply fearful of rejection, super-sensitised to perceived criticism, embarrassment or hostility; and in the close commu-nity atmosphere, with my strong patterns of self-judgement, these emotions reappeared frequently. My body could be thrown into a rage after hearing a single comment that I thought was unfair, and I would watch helplessly as my stomach crumpled and my mind began spinning with thoughts of blame or revenge. On other occasions, the impulse to run and hide could be similarly overwhelming.

What comes up in contemplative life is sometimes described as 'manure for the mind'. It might not always smell great; but given the right handling, it promotes cultivation. When a group of people share physical and psychic space for twenty-four hours a day, week after week, there is no getting away from yourself or others. As in every other human community, conflicts arise – perhaps more so in a group of strangers from twenty countries who have chosen to live in close proximity, often despite having little in common aside from a shared commitment to meditation. Nevertheless, because of this commitment, emotive disagreements help each person to work with their habits and recognise old patterns of thought, feeling and behaviour. They also provide opportunities to communicate with as much awareness, compassion and skill as can be found. The shared commitment to being genuine and gentle means most conflicts can be resolved, even among those who come from very different backgrounds and have contrasting mindsets. The principles and practices of mindfulness can be guiding stars – no matter how far one's vision strays from them, they remain constant, something to return to (just like the breath during meditation practice) after a time of wandering.

In this environment, I deepened my capacity to offer space to the reactions of my mind and body, neither acting them out nor repressing or running from them. As I watched, I noticed a pattern of angry resistance mutating into an accepting sadness. And if I stayed open to this experience, rather than walling myself off, my body would start to soften. Perhaps then I'd find a space in a far corner of the land, sitting on a tree stump where I couldn't be heard, and let go into crying. If I practised allowing space for difficult feelings, I learned that they would eventually pass.

Gradually, as I continued to train in meditation, this new approach to working with feelings became more familiar. Rather than trying to analyse them with thinking, distract from them with activity, or get annoyed with them for being there at all, I learned to allow these experiences, to hold them gently in awareness and watch them as they mutated in their own time. This wasn't easy, but it generated far less stress than my previous attempts to resist them. And when the difficult feelings dissolved, I was often left with contentment.

This happened repeatedly during my year at Dechen Choling. It wasn't particularly pleasant, but it *was* transformative. I got to see my habits up close and often. Unpleasant thoughts and sensations would appear, and I'd feel a strong urge to struggle or resist. As I refused to act on that urge, energy would well up in me even more. But eventually, like a breaking wave, the intensity would pass, crashing out with the water of my tears.

Sometimes the trigger for one of these episodes would come from a memory, as if space had been created in my formerly crowded mind for the past to be processed. A thought of an old regret or loss would appear, along with associated feelings of aching, tightening, bursting or heaviness. Letting the memory emerge with the feelings, without needing to follow the thoughts that accompanied it, many old ghosts were laid to rest. Old hurts and resentments were transformed into acceptance simply through the process of feeling and acknowledging them. Grief, over time, transformed into peace.

As I became more familiar with this pattern, I was increasingly able to stay present at the moment of strongest impulse. Unlike at home – where I could easily isolate, distract or lose myself in busyness – there was nowhere to go, except into the local coun-tryside. Before long, the château bell would call me back for my daily tasks, meditation or a meal. It sometimes felt excruciating to return, as I sensed (perhaps mistakenly) that pain was etched on my face and body, inviting the scrutiny of others. But I could also feel that something was changing in my approach to facing difficulty. Rather than trying to avoid it, and ending up feeling dominated, I was practising *being* with it and discovering that the negative thoughts and sensations dissolved more quickly than when I reacted with panic or withdrawal. I could gently anchor my attention to the flow of breath in my body and work to stay open and present. Over time, with lots of practice, this became easier to do. The muscle of mindfulness was growing within me. The reactive habit of anxiety and depression was starting to lose some of its power.

There was no turning away from this path now. Even if it were possible to close the lid on awareness, I wasn't prepared to do it. I had glimpsed some sparkling treasures, and the costs of shutdown would be more than I was prepared to pay. Time on earth seemed too short and precious to waste on chasing after petty pleasures. In any case, these now seemed flat and tasteless when compared to the multidimensional insights that came from meditation.

The principles and practices of Buddhism were starting to provide a real grounding for me. I was developing genuine confidence in this way of life, and sometimes I was even able to embody it. The practices increasingly seemed to lead to competence – a capacity to handle life more deftly. This was empowering in itself. A virtuous cycle was developing. Previously, stress had led to fear and the belief that I couldn't cope; now, I was more able to meet difficulties with a sense of trust that I'd be able to manage.

Nevertheless, retreat life remained a challenge. There was rarely any respite from the intensity and intimacy of daily experience. There were hundreds of practitioners during the summer, and it was the job of the staff to care for them. This could be joyful, but it was also tiring. Many of those who stayed long term lived off the land, or at least had their own rooms. By contrast, there was little personal space or privacy for those of us who shared accommodation, and fatigue was a common problem. Everyone was committed to a life of service, but this isn't always easy with no door to close at the end of the day.

I remained at Dechen Choling for the whole of 2006, but as winter set in, I sensed a change. My commitment to meditation was unwavering, but I wasn't sure that retreat life was the best way for me to express it at this time. I had learned a lot from living so closely with others, but repeating the calendar in 2007 could have become a new kind of hiding for me. Just as I had in the months before leaving England, I started feeling lethargic, irritated and resistant to the routines of everyday life. When I tried to deny what my insides were telling me, the stress mounted. Fortunately, my meditation practice had taught me to listen to my body, and the message was coming through loud and clear. I had already arranged a visit to England, and when I arrived I felt – and accepted – a strong sense of relief. This was confirmation – it was time to go home.

But what would I do once I was there? There were few day jobs involving meditation, yet this way of life had become central for me – committing to anything else now felt too compromising. I considered going back to academic life, as a Buddhist Studies Ph.D. student. But as someone who was prone to living in his head, I was concerned about the dryness of academia. Perhaps it would be just another kind of hiding. Dechen Choling was inspirational because it was a container for practice, a lived embodiment of mind, body and culture. I knew that this was possible in rural France, but something told me that it must be possible in the midst of mainstream society, too. I just needed a way to find and express it.

In the meantime, though, I needed money. Having brushed up on my French and Spanish, my brother found me work translating texts, while I mined old contacts for writing and editing jobs. A short stint working at a drug rehab centre reminded me that traditional therapeutic work wasn't for me, and I figured that until I found something with meditation at its heart, it would be best to stay freelance. This enabled me to build my work around meditation practice.

As I reconstructed a life at home, I realised that things had truly changed over the previous year. While this latest set of transitions wasn't easy, I was negotiating them with a degree of gentleness, patience and perseverance that had been beyond me a few years before. Within the space of a few months, I moved house several times and started a number of different jobs. I was living in a state of uncertainty – financial, geographical, vocational – but I didn't fall into depression (despite some difficult days and weeks).

For the most part, I meditated for an hour or two each day. I did my best to bring what I'd learned of impermanence into the rapidly shifting sands of my life. The future felt unsure, but for perhaps the first time in my life, that seemed okay. The episodes of crying that had continued throughout my year at Dechen Choling had now largely abated.

As part of my search for work, I contacted the Mental Health Foundation and was surprised to hear that they wanted me back. As well as helping with a major ongoing project – exploring the causes of and potential remedies for anxiety – they invited me to pitch new ideas. I wondered whether there was some way I could persuade them to look into meditation. Emboldened by the confidence my practice had given me, I embarked on some investigative research.

The internet brought results I hadn't expected. At Bangor University, there was a department called the Centre for Mindfulness Research and Practice. It had been set up by Professor Mark Williams, who together with his colleagues John Teasdale and Zindel Segal had developed a meditation-based course to help protect people who were prone to depression. Not only did their programme produce some very good results – a 40–50 per cent reduction in relapse rates – but they had tested it in high-quality clinical trials. The evidence was sufficiently strong that their course, Mindfulness-Based Cognitive Therapy (MBCT) was recommended by the National Institute for Health and Clinical Excellence

(NICE; now known as the National Institute for Health and Care Excellence) for people who had experienced multiple episodes of depression.

In the UK, inclusion in the NICE guidelines is a green light for offering treatments in the National Health Service. This seemed remarkable, even to me, who knew how effective meditation could be. NICE didn't view the practice as an alternative or religious approach, but as an evidence-based healthcare intervention. As I searched more deeply, I also discovered – to my surprise– that Mark Williams had recently moved to Oxford, where he had set up a new mindfulness centre. Oxford University had a centre devoted to mindfulness, not as part of a Buddhist Studies programme, but within the Department of Psychology! It was already working in partnership with local health service trusts.

A few weeks before I left London for Dechen Choling, a friend who knew about my struggles with depression had picked a book off his shelf and suggested I read it. It was about six hundred pages long, with a blue cover adorned with white mountain peaks. It had an unusual title – *Full Catastrophe Living*[2] – and the author's name was Dr Jon Kabat-Zinn. Apparently, Kabat-Zinn had developed a meditation programme that he taught to patients suffering from chronic pain at a hospital in Massachusetts. The course was called Mindfulness-Based Stress Reduction (MBSR) and it was designed to help patients manage the difficulties of long-term illness.

My friend also put on one of Kabat-Zinn's meditation CDs. I lay down while the doctor led me through a practice called the body scan, which involved paying attention to sensations in different parts of the body, region by region. I was in a state of high anxiety at the time, so I didn't really connect to the practice. Still, I took the book home and read it from cover to cover. It told the stories of patients with serious conditions who had found some peace through Kabat-Zinn's programme. Curiously, although everything described in *Full Catastrophe Living* seemed congruent with Buddhist approaches, there was little or no mention of Buddhism in the book. Exactly the same principles and practices were presented, but with somewhat different emphases in terminology. Specifically, Kabat-Zinn kept returning to the word 'mindfulness', which he defined as 'paying attention in a particular way, on purpose, in the present moment, and non-judgementally'. This, he explained, was cultivated through the practice of meditation, and by embodying a set of attitudes (such as acceptance, curiosity and letting go) that could bring about a reduction in stress. It was clear that Kabat-Zinn's programme was deeply informed by the Buddhist tradition, yet, by using non-religious language, he was successfully transmitting its core messages and practices in a Western hospital setting, connecting with people who'd be unlikely ever to set foot in a Buddhist centre.

When I first read *Full Catastrophe Living*, my mind had already moved on from the relationship between meditation and medicine. I had decided to commit myself to Buddhist training in a Buddhist setting, so, while Kabat-Zinn's approach was intriguing, I didn't give it much further thought. But now I was back in the UK, I could see how some aspects of Buddhist teaching and terminology could prevent its benefits from reaching a wider audience. For instance, along with the practical training in how to work with the mind and body, Buddhism is often wrapped in a worldview that points to an existence beyond this plane – multiple lifetimes in multiple realms.

Personally, I had found opening to these perspectives helpful. The possibility of life beyond the immediately apparent allowed me to develop a sense of space, and of wonder, and helped me to realise that day-to-day troubles might not matter so much. While I tended to resist dogma whenever presented as fact, I enjoyed the process of exploring the mysteries of existence. As Lady Caithness said, claiming to quote Voltaire: 'It is no more surprising to be born twice than to be born once.'[3] But belief is not required to engender wonder. Just looking at the sea or the stars, marvelling at the weirdness of night-time dreams, or contemplating the miracle of being conscious in a human body, with all its amazing constituents, is enough to invoke a sense of awe that can change one's perspective on mundane problems. The key to tuning in to this sense of amazement, it seemed to me, was a willingness to pay attention, to look at, listen to and feel the everyday magic of the world – to make the most of *being* alive. As Coleman Barks, translator of the poet Rumi puts it: 'Just being sentient and in a body with the sun coming up is a state of rapture.'[4]

As I delved into the research on 'mindfulness-based approaches', I came across the work of Kabat-Zinn again. His stress-reduction programme had been the model for Williams, Teasdale and Segal's MBCT course, and most of the evidence on the usefulness of meditation for promoting good mental and physical health was based on either MBSR or MBCT. Now I could really understand why Kabat-Zinn's work was so skilful. He had extracted the essentials of Buddhist training from the belief systems and Eastern cultural forms that tended to accompany them, and had offered them, simply but precisely, within a framework that many more Westerners – be they atheists, agnostics or non-Buddhist religious believers – were likely to accept.

Western practitioners adopted Buddhist practices widely in the 1960s and 1970s – the hippie era of experimentation. This association stuck as the mainstream tended to label anyone who meditated as counter-cultural, new-age, credulous or even immature or self-indulgent. The idea that meditation might be taught to patients in traditional hospitals would have been laughable at the time. This was the backdrop to which Kabat-Zinn developed MBSR in the late 1970s. He had trained with several Buddhist teachers, but also knew that the forms and settings in which meditation was usually practised would restrict its adoption in conventional healthcare systems. Nevertheless, as a molecular biologist working at the University of Massachusetts Medical School, he also believed that these principles and practices could provide significant relief to some of the patients. Often enduring both chronic pain and the stress that accompanies living with a long-term condition – and in the absence of a quick-fix medical solution – these patients faced years of suffering. By offering them ways to understand and work mindfully with their experience, Kabat-Zinn felt that their loads could be lightened.

So, rather than gathering in a Buddhist retreat, participants in Kabat-Zinn's MBSR programme met in the UMass hospital basement. There was no talk of past or future lives or different realms, and no ancient Sanskrit terminology. Instead, there was an uncompromising focus on the basic training that Buddhists have long found leads to the relief of suffering. In eight weekly sessions and a single one-day retreat, Kabat-Zinn led his students through the foundations of this 'mindfulness' training. Between sessions, he asked them to practise body scans, sitting meditation and mindful movement practices such as yoga for around forty-five minutes every day.

A scientist by training, Kabat-Zinn knew it was vital to study the effects of his programme. Gradually, through this research, a picture began to emerge of experience being transformed. Early trials suggested that patients felt less troubled by pain, and less anxious, after mindfulness training.[5] Through his research, writings and a US TV documentary that aired in the early 1990s, Kabat-Zinn came to the attention of other healthcare practitioners and scientists. Among them were Williams, Teasdale and Segal, who had been funded to develop a version of cognitive-behavioural therapy that could be offered to help people – like me – who were prone to depression. They realised that mindfulness, as taught by Kabat-Zinn, helped patients cultivate a different relationship with their stress and pain, and wondered if it could also help people who suffer from depression to disentangle themselves from the thoughts and emotions that drag them into despair.

Their work led to the development of MBCT, an eight-week programme of meditation based on MBSR, and the research that convinced NICE to recommend it. But although it was included in the guidelines for preventing recurring depression, MBCT was not a well-known approach when I first came across it. In 2008, the chances of a referral to an NHS mindfulness programme were minimal.

Having discovered the credibility of mindfulness as a treatment for recurrent depression, I suggested that the Mental Health Foundation might explore it further. As an evidence-based, NICE-recommended approach that was nevertheless rarely available, there was clearly a gap to be filled. To my delight, the foundation not only supported the idea but found someone to pay for it. A private sponsor with experience of meditation was looking to fund some charity work, and this project fitted the bill perfectly. In January 2009, I started work on a report with the intention of setting out the arguments for offering mindfulness more widely.

During this work, I accessed meditation in new ways. First of all, I immersed myself in studies that assessed the benefits of mindfulness, from which a clear and consistent picture emerged.[6] The research pointed to mindfulness being a healthy way to approach life. People who are more mindful are less likely than others to experience psychological distress, they are less neurotic and generally happier with their lives. They are also less likely to get stuck in negative thought patterns, are more aware and accepting of their emotions, are less impulsive, and recover from low moods more quickly, as well as having more control over their behaviour. They are less likely to try to avoid the inevitable difficulties of life. Instead, they have what's called an 'approach mentality' – willing to explore and work with challenges, without expecting to do everything perfectly.

More mindful people have greater self-esteem and an internally generated sense of confidence. They are better able to express themselves in social situations, are more sensitive to and understanding of others, and are less socially anxious and less negatively affected by the emotions of those around them. All of this makes them better communicators and better able to overcome relationship difficulties, as well as more compassionate to themselves and others.

In short, the studies suggested that mindful people are not only happier but more capable, caring and confident.

The research also indicated that mindfulness can be practised by almost anyone. After taking a mindfulness course, usually over a couple of months, many participants experienced significant changes in their lives. Mindfulness-trained people are less likely to fall into anxiety and depression as they get caught up less often in repetitive, negative thoughts. They are more able to regulate their emotions, being less blown about by the difficulties of life and the extreme feelings that challenging circumstances evoke. They have greater psychological health and well-being, less stress, and tend to feel more engaged and energised.

There are benefits to physical health, too. Given a flu vaccine after a mindfulness course, participants responded with stronger antibody responses than a control group, suggesting that their immune systems had been boosted. In general, people trained in mindfulness report fewer symptoms of whatever illnesses they experience, visit the doctor less often and are more able to cope with any condition. Stress hormone levels in the body become lower, too.

Addictive patterns, such as overeating or smoking, become weaker with mindfulness. And the quality of people's connections improve. Couples trained in mindfulness become more satisfied with their relationships, closer to and more accepting of their partners, and more able to cope with conflict. Sleep, relaxation, concentration, empathy – whatever aspect of well-being is tested, mindfulness training seems to improve it. I once heard it described as like WD40 for well-being – a small amount unlocks a lot of doors.

People's brains change when they learn mindfulness. After an eight-week course, participants display a shift in activity from the right to left pre-frontal cortex, correlating with less anxiety and depression, and with more of an 'approach mentality'. Thickening in regions of the brain associated with memory, emotion regulation, self-awareness and perspective-taking has also been recorded, as well as reduced activity and density in the amygdala – a part of the limbic system that is known to be more active in people who are prone to mood disorders.

The brain changes in response to experience – a phenomenon known as neuroplasticity. It's a bit like going to the gym – when you train your body with weights and intense cardiovascular activity, the body responds over time with larger muscles and greater fitness. When we train the mind in meditation, it seems we hone its fitness to work with the events of our lives. With exercise, the results can be felt and seen in body shape and physical capacity. With meditation, the results can be experienced in our changing relationship with life, and – if you happen to have an fMRI scanner – through observable shifts in neural activity and structure.

Everything that happens in life is experienced in the mind and the body. Thus, it makes sense to learn how to use these instruments effectively, because how we perceive, relate to and respond to events determine, to a large extent, the quality of our experience. My research suggested that a relatively short period of meditation training, practised in a mainstream setting, could effect significant changes that would help people to manage their lives more skilfully, and so reduce their stress and suffering.

Alongside the research, I wanted to experience the approach first hand. While much of what I read about MBSR and MBCT was familiar from my own Buddhist training, I was curious about many aspects of the two programmes. In particular, I wondered how it was possible to distil the core Buddhist teachings on working with the mind into just eight two-hour sessions. How could such expansive wisdom, which invites us to consider the very foundations of how we experience our lives, be presented so simply – and seemingly so effectively – in terms that would make sense to someone with no experience of – or interest in – the Buddhist tradition? To find out, I enrolled as a participant in one course of MBCT and one of MBSR. Initially, my motivation for taking the two courses was to bring further insights into my research and report. But gradually, as my understanding of the model deepened, I began to develop a profound appreciation of how mindfulness was taught and practised on these courses – simply, and precisely.

It had been nearly a decade since I had first started meditating, and seven years since I had begun a daily practice, and I now knew that it was the most important skill I'd ever learned. My life had gradually shifted from wild rushing around and grasping for pleasure, to panicked struggling to escape pain, and finally into a greater groundedness, within which I felt more present, centred and in touch. I was more able to hold events, thoughts and sensations in awareness, and so be less in thrall to them. My actions tended to be chosen, rather than automatic. The world felt mysterious, open and interesting, rather than frightening, overpowering and claustrophobic.

It had been a period of great change, with the many shifts in job and location reflecting the major deconstruction and rebuilding that had been going on inside me. Sometimes it was hard for me to believe that I had once been the deputy editor of *FHM*, and was now an advocate for meditation in the health service. My own practice had started when I was in a frozen-solid depression of almost three years' duration. Now the periods of struggle in the darkness were much more short-lived, while the times of remission – both within episodes and between them – were becoming ever stronger and longer.

I was convinced that working with the awareness found in my practice was the key to well-being in my life. But I also understood that aspects of traditional Buddhism would be problematic for many people in Western society. A more mainstream mindfulness approach offered a way to bridge the gap: a practical, experiential training in meditation that helped people to understand and work with their minds, bodies and lives, and brought relief from suffering.

The Buddha is sometimes referred to as a great physician, and the training he outlined is often described as medicine, rather than religion. On the basis of both the first-person evidence of what we experience with our own senses and the third-person evidence of scientific research, I felt that MBSR and MBCT offered a pragmatic approach that was completely within the spirit of this framework. These two mindfulness-based programmes were bringing these practical teachings lucidly into the twenty-first-century Western world.

It also gradually dawned on me that I now had an opportunity to make meditation the centre of my life's activities, while still remaining within the mainstream world. Following the publication of the *Be Mindful* report, which recommended making mindfulness more widely available within the National Health Service – especially for people who are prone to depression – I went on a mindfulness teacher-training retreat at the Centre for Mindfulness Research and Practice, Bangor University. I've been teaching mindfulness courses ever since.

Practice to try: Body scan

Body scanning is a foundational practice of most mindfulness courses. Although my first experience of it was neither easy nor pleasant, I have come, over time, to see it as a brilliant way to tune to presence. While often practised lying down, it's important to recognise that the body scan is not a relaxation exercise – the point is not to feel calm (and particularly not to try to feel calm). The prime intention of a body scan is to incline the mind into sensory experience – to become aware of how it is to 'be a body'. What we discover when we do this – mind wandering, tension, anxiety, boredom, peace, stillness, contentment, numbness, discomfort, irritation – is less important than our willingness to work with these arising phenomena gently and patiently, coming back to friendly attention each time we notice that the mind has drifted into thinking, or is buying into attachment or aversion. It can be especially helpful to practise the body scan with an attitude of 'abandoning all hope of fruition'. Just like a scientist, see if you can carry out the experiment of the practice and explore whatever results occur.

Below are some guidelines for practising a body scan. However, the best way to practise is with audio guidance. There's a guided body scan audio, led by me, in the set available at www.edhalliwell.com.

1. Lie down on a comfortable and preferably firm surface – a
    mat or blanket on the floor is good. Allow your body to sink
    into the ground underneath. This is an opportunity for you
    to let go for a time, to drop into stillness, to feel yourself
    being held by the earth. Close your eyes (if that feels okay
    for you) and invite a sense of presence by opening your
    awareness to the sensations of the body on the ground – the
    texture of the blanket or mat or your clothes, the heaviness
    and warmth of your body. Are these sensations the same
    right through the body, or different in various locations?
    Invite a friendly curiosity to your experience. For instance,
    you could ask, 'How does it feel to be lying here right
    now?' There is no right or wrong answer to this question –
    noticing what you're sensing is what matters.

2. Bring your attention now to breathing, feeling the rising and
    falling of inhalation and exhalation, wherever you are feeling
    it. Imagine that you're dropping anchor into the breath, your
    attention placed gently on the rhythm of breathing, and allow
    your mind to settle into its pattern, riding the waves of the
    breath as air ebbs and flows within you. At any time during
    the body scan practice, you can 'drop anchor' into the breath
    as a way of regrounding, resettling into your centre.

3. On an outbreath, let go of attending to the breath and drop
    your attention into your left leg, moving your mind's eye
    down into the left foot, and coming to rest in the left big toe.
    Notice what sensations, if any, are present in the left big toe
    right now. There's no need to do anything with them – just
    observe them, let them be felt. If no sensations are present,
    notice what the absence is like. Be aware of changes in
    sensation, and any tendency to try to hold on to them or
    push them away.

4. If you like, synchronise your sensing with the rhythm of your breath by breathing 'into' the left big toe on each in-breath, and breathing 'out from' the toe on each out-breath.

5. Now move your mind to each of the other toes of the left foot in turn, giving each a few moments of attention. Be interested in the changing experience as you move your mind through the toes.

6. You will probably notice thoughts and reactions arising as you practise. This isn't a problem, and there's no need to try to alter or get rid of them. At the same time, as we're practising paying attention to body sensations in a particular part of the body, allow yourself to let go of following these thoughts and reactions. See if you can just let them be there in the background of your experience. When you notice your attention has wandered into thought, or is following an impulse, or has drifted to a different part of the body, you might acknowledge that this wandering has occurred, then gently return your attention to the toes.

7. Open your awareness now to the top of the left foot, resting with sensations in this region for a while. Now offer a friendly presence to the bottom of the foot, and to the heel. Gradually work your way up through the left leg (ankle, lower leg, knee and so on), giving your attention over to whatever sensations arise in the region you have reached. After arriving at the top of the left leg, drop the attention down into the right big toe, and gradually scan through that foot and leg, too.

8. Gently and carefully work your attention through the whole body in this way (hips, pelvic region, back, shoulders,

each arm and hand, belly, chest, neck and head). Gently acknowledge mind wandering when you notice it, and let this be an opportunity to practise kindness, patience and conscious choice, as you bring the attention back to any sensations in the region of the body you are working with.

9. Practise working the muscle of mindfulness, not just by coming back when you notice the mind has wandered, but by playing with both a wider and a narrower focus of attention. In some regions of the body, experiment with moving in close to a particular part (such as a finger or an eyelid); at other times, expand to a wider perspective (such as attending to the whole of the back, a leg, or the head).

10. When you have scanned the entire body, let your attention open out to notice all of your body's sensations, and let them be held in kindly awareness. Perhaps imagine that you are breathing into the whole body as each in-breath happens, and breathing out from the whole body with each out-breath. Rest in this open awareness of all body sensations for several moments before opening your eyes, stretching and gently getting up. See if you can maintain this sense of whole-body awareness as you move through the next phase of your day.

Seven aspects of mindfulness trained in the body scan

Although in some ways it can seem quite simple, mindfulness is a multifaceted skill. The body scan

is a great starting practice because it fundamentally
trains so many aspects of working skilfully with
experience. Here are seven aspects of mindfulness
that are practised in the body scan. We will explore
each more closely in the forthcoming chapters.

- **Attention.** By consciously choosing to place the
  mind on an object, we are training our capacity to
  pay attention. Attention is also trained by moving
  the mind from one object to another, and by
  coming back to an object when we notice the mind
  has wandered. Training attention in a body scan is
  a bit like doing resistance work in the gym – it takes
  some effort, but it cultivates strength and flexibility.
  Remember, each time you practise a body scan, you
  are strengthening the muscles of mindfulness.

- **Awareness.** When they first practise the body
  scan, most people notice that their mind seems to
  roam all over the place. We intend to pay attention
  consistently, but that's not quite what happens.
  This is not a problem – part of the practice is to
  bring awareness to whatever is happening in the
  mind, even if it's not exactly what we'd like it to be.
  Knowing our patterns is the first step to working
  with them skilfully. With awareness, we are open
  to the landscape of the mind, able to see the terrain
  of our being.

- **Embodiment.** Repeatedly bringing attention to our
  bodies balances the tendency to 'live in our heads'.

The body senses rather than thinks, so, by allowing body sensations to be felt, we can drop into a fuller sensory palette. Living from our bodies, we tune into a mode of perceiving that's more centred, grounded and directly in touch with the world around us, rather than always getting caught up in concepts.

- **Letting be.** Many of us are used to driving ourselves hard. We think of training as a way to try to force change, push, pull, cajole and badger ourselves into becoming something different. Mindfulness training encourages a different approach. Each time we come back to attention in the body scan, it's suggested we do so gently. When we notice the mind is wandering, we do so with acceptance – this is just the way the mind is, for now. While we may not always like what we find, we can practise allowing it as our starting point, rather than trying to resist it or try to force change, which just creates struggle and stress.

- **Approaching.** As we move into body sensations, we may discover feelings that we don't like. Discomfort and pain, irritation and boredom, sadness and numbness are all common experiences for people practising a body scan. Our usual way of meeting these sensations is to try not to meet them – to escape from their unpleasantness by distracting from, ruminating on, or battling with them. Sometimes, though, there isn't anything

we can do to make them go away on demand –
physical or emotional pain tends not to listen to
reason. So, rather than exacerbating our misery
by struggling with it, the body scan teaches us
how to lean gently into discomfort. Although this
seems counter-intuitive, it reduces the unwelcome
sensations' power to derail us. When we approach
our experience with interest, although we may
feel unpleasant sensations fully, we also drop our
attachment to the stressful thoughts and reactions
that are typically layered on top of them.

- **Appreciation.** It's easy to go through life taking
  things for granted. But contemplate this for a
  moment. Isn't it amazing that we have a body at all,
  and a mind to experience it? By paying attention
  to body sensations, and noticing what arises in
  awareness, we incline our interest into being alive,
  not as a set of philosophical ideas, but as actual
  phenomena – the very experience of things. This
  enables us to tune into the actuality of moment-by-
  moment living, generating appreciation that can
  nurture a sense of awe and gratitude.

- **Getting unstuck.** When we pay attention with
  mindfulness, we come to observe and feel the
  reality that everything is always changing. We
  notice how stress arises when we try to hold on to
  pleasant sensations and/or reject painful ones, and
  we see how sensations are moving, shifting, rising
  and falling in intensity all the time. We may even

see how we are no longer so caught up in ourselves when we drop our sense of fixed identity ('My leg hurts!') and invite an awareness of the aspects and processes of experience ('There is an ache right now, and a thought about that ache'). Getting unstuck from mistaken assumptions about how things are – and how we are – can start to bring some relief.

CHAPTER FOUR

If the Heart Wanders . . .

If the heart wanders or is distracted, bring it
back to the point quite gently, and even if you
do nothing during the whole of your hour
but bring your heart back a thousand times,
though it went away every time you brought it
back, your hour would be very well employed.

Francis De Sales[1]

'Pay attention!' was a refrain I remember hearing often at school. Whether the lesson was maths, English, art, geography or PE, there was an implicit understanding that learning requires being focused on the subject at hand. However, I don't remember ever being taught *how* to pay attention. We were just told to do it. Despite thousands of hours of formal education, there was no exploration of the processes of consciousness. We thought and we did. But we weren't invited to look at how this happened, or to consider whether there might be an art to working with experience.

Reflecting back, this seems astonishing. How can we learn to live life well if we spend our whole time caught up in our thoughts and feelings, without understanding how they occur? Despite being the means through which every event in life is felt and interpreted, patterns of sensing and thinking are generally left unexamined.

Even while studying for a history degree at Cambridge University, supposedly one of the top educational institutions in the world, there was little contemplation of the processes of consciousness. In my first term, I remember being told that we would be 'turned into intellectuals', but it seemed this would happen without learning much about the intellect itself (let alone sensory experiences in the body). We were encouraged to do lots of thinking, but we didn't learn about the mind.

Our brains and bodies comprise some of the most sophisticated equipment in the known universe. And yet we are never given a manual that explains how they work; and most of us devote little time to finding out. Some of us still get along okay, some of the time, but wouldn't it help to take a look at ourselves, to make sense of the tools we've been given? Buddhist psychology was a revelation for me because it was like stumbling on a manual for the mind. The instructions said that in order to experience contentment, you had to examine the workings of perception. In other words, you have to watch – and learn from – your experience. The manual also taught an efficient method for this investigation – mindfulness meditation shows us how to look.

Courses like Mindfulness-Based Stress Reduction and Mindfulness-Based Cognitive Therapy draw on this method, backing it up with findings from modern disciplines such as evolutionary psychology, stress physiology and neuroscience. The more I practised and taught from this framework, the more I came to appreciate its directness and precision. Secular and evidence-based, the mainstream mindfulness approach offers a skilful way to investigate how our minds and bodies work, and to see if there's a way to manage them better.

What do we find when we practise meditation, such as mindfulness of breathing or the body scan? The first thing most of us discover is that our attention wanders away, again and again, without our intending that to happen. We mean to stay focused on a single thing – the flow of breath, sensations in the body, or even making and drinking a cup of tea – but before we know it, we've drifted somewhere else. No matter how much we resolve to stay present to the chosen object, distraction keeps happening. It soon dawns that we're as much slave to as master of our own mind.

How is this happening? In Buddhist psychology, events and our relationships with them are described as arising through the process of the five *skandhas* – form, feeling, perception, inclination and consciousness (see Chapter 2). An event happens (form) and we experience it through one or more of our sense organs, which produces a sensation in the body (feeling). Usually unconsciously, the feeling is categorised as pleasant, unpleasant or neutral (perception). If it is neutral, the event may be ignored, but if it's either pleasant or unpleasant, we are prompted into thoughts, emotions, attitudes and urges (inclination), which draw us towards taking action. Consciousness, the fifth *skandha*, makes everything available to experience.

Stress arises because the perceptions and concepts that arise in relation to events and our sensory experiences of them are habitually laced with craving (or its alter-ego, aversion). Something happens, and the feeling it produces is met with either wanting the experience or not wanting it. We are thus either drawn to try to perpetuate that experience, if we find it pleasant, or are repelled from it, if we find it unpleasant. Our thoughts, emotions and behaviour all reflect this basic reaction. We are rarely fully present to an experience, instead getting stuck in distraction and struggle that is stressful. We are constantly busy, constantly agitated, constantly daydreaming.

Often, events in life seem to happen so quickly and unconsciously that the *skandhas* seem all tangled together – just a big mess of happenings, impulses, thinking and reaction. Sensations and thoughts spin off immediately from any given stimulus, propelled by habit, and before we know it we have done something without knowing why or how. It's like we're operating in a kind of waking sleep, propelled through our days unconsciously, on autopilot. The bad news is that strong conditioning forces lie behind these processes. Thoughts, emotions and reactions all arise with such powerful energy that we are often not aware of them until they are already happening or sometimes until after they have happened. The mind, in one memorable Buddhist description, is like a drunken monkey that's been bitten by a scorpion – constantly leaping from tree to tree in a crazed bid to find contentment and avoid displeasure. In this frantic state, impelled by the search for happiness, we often don't even realise that we are out of control.

However, there's good news, too. With training, we can start to work with this situation. If we practise noticing and distinguishing aspects of experience as they happen, as well as our reactions to them, the arising of experience can start to be seen more consciously. As soon as we realise how much the mind wanders, we are already on the path to freedom. We are starting to notice how events in the mind, body and environment all interact with one another, producing the experience of our lives. With practice, we can become familiar with how automatic reactions of attachment and avoidance come about, and see how they create stressful effects. Simply observing how mind wandering happens is the start of this process, because seeing our habits in motion already allows us to be less caught up in them, and less driven by them.

Unconscious life is like being caught on a revolving hamster wheel, propelled by our own activity. Meditation offers the possibility of relief by inviting us to step off the wheel for a while. From a place of relative stillness, we can experience the wheel's turning from a new perspective. By removing our conscious energy from it, we're no longer increasing the speed of its spin. Everything can slow down a little, which makes observation easier. We might feel quite dizzy stepping off at first, but in time this will ease, too.

In mindfulness meditation, connecting with the breath and the body allows us to step onto steadier ground and experience life from a different place. When people notice their busyness in meditation, it's a sign that they are starting to observe what happens in the mind and the body, perhaps for the first time, without being carried away by its momentum. Most of us seem to need a practice to help us see what's really going on, because the compulsion to engage in thinking and activity is extremely strong. One recent study found that, when asked to sit still without any external distractions for fifteen minutes, many people (67 per cent of men and 25 per cent of women) preferred to give themselves an electric shock rather than complete the experiment. All of the volunteers had previously stated that they would be willing to pay five dollars not to experience the shock.[2] But when it came to sitting still with their minds, the compulsion to do something – even something they knew would hurt – propelled them to act.

Understandings of experience based on modern research correlate closely with ancient Buddhist models of the mind. Descriptions of the five *skandhas*, leading to the experience of suffering through clinging and aversion, are not so different from researchers' findings in relation to the processes of human perception and reaction. It seems that observing the mind through scientific study produces insights that are congruent with watching the mind in meditation.

In his research, Matt Killingsworth at Harvard University has found that distraction is indeed very common – his data reveal that we do not pay attention to what we're doing 47 per cent of the time.[3] Left to its own devices, the mind repeatedly flies off into thinking and analysis, repeatedly going over what's happened, is happening or might happen. Rather than focusing on actual experience, the mind gets caught in judgements, ideas, fantasies and ruminations.

There are benefits to having a wandering mind. The capacity to think outside of basic sensory experience – what is sometimes called 'the rolling present' – enables us to plan for the future, solve abstract problems, reflect and learn from mistakes. This seems to be part of what sets humans apart from other animals, and it's certainly been a crucial element in the process of civilisation. At some point, our ancestors decided it would be a good idea to plant seeds, rather than eat them all as and when they found them. This was a choice that required considered reflection and analysis ('I saw seeds grow into plants') as well as patience and forethought ('I want to eat this seed right now, but it could grow into a plant, feeding me and others for much longer, as long as I'm willing to refrain from my impulse to eat it immediately'). This was the start of agriculture. Mind wandering allows for many kinds of learning and creativity, from which numerous human achievements have stemmed.

But there are costs, too. The second thing many of us notice when we begin a meditation practice is that our mind wanders into states of dissatisfaction more often than it moves into states of well-being. We sit down to practise, perhaps hoping for happiness and calm, and find our attention drawn to aches and pains, or difficult emotions, or negative patterns of thought. Along with abstract conceptualisation comes the possibility of regret and worry.

When a lion runs at a group of antelopes, then catches and kills one, the rest of the herd will generally regroup a bit further away, shake themselves down, and carry on grazing. They don't seem greatly tormented by what's just happened. You can imagine what would happen if the antelopes had human minds and brains. Soon after the attack was over, thoughts would start whirring in the survivors' minds: 'Phew! I escaped the lion. Wait a minute, though.

There are *loads* of lions around here. There'll be another one coming along soon. Oh, this is terrible, I'm not safe at all here. But there's nowhere I can go. I'll end up like poor Archie – a lion's lunch! It's awful being an antelope. And I'll really miss Archie. What was the last thing I said to him? I think I told him he was looking a bit chubby. That wasn't very nice, was it? I'm a terrible antelope – insulting my mate just before he was eaten by a lion!'

By now, rather than calmly grazing, the antelope with a human mind is having heart palpitations. With a churning stomach and muscles locked in tension, its body is stuck in a state of high alert – a stress reaction that would be useful if another lion actually were hunting for food near by, but in this case one that was triggered by its human mind's ability to wander out of the present moment and ruminate on thoughts, rather than just grass. The antelope's stress reactions are produced as much from its relationship with events as from the events themselves. With a human mind, unpleasant events aren't just painful – they produce stress reactions based on the *mental interpretation* of those events, rather than just the *sensory experience* of them.

If we identify strongly with negative thoughts and emotions, we are more likely to get stressed.[4] Our immune system may be impaired, and we'll be more prone to illness. Our interpretations of and reactions to events can lead to unhappiness and illness that don't seem to be shared by seemingly less conscious animals. The antelope with an antelope's mind may have a more limited experience of life, but it probably gets less stressed than any human.

Ultimately, escaping the lot of the antelope – stuck in unawareness, vulnerable to lion attack – requires a mind that can reflect on the painful possibilities of being eaten, and plan some means of protection. Rumination and worry – plus the body sensations that often accompany them – are powerful tools for survival and, primed by evolution, they operate automatically. Unfortunately, though, they are not very pleasant, so the price of survival is discontent. Matt Killingsworth found that people are a lot less happy during and after mind wandering. In fact, the relationship between happiness and distractedness is quite a lot stronger than the relationship between happiness and wealth.

Even more unfortunate is that the mind tends to wander into a partial – and often inaccurate – version of events. The mind has evolved a range of heuristics – perceptual biases – that consistently affect our interpretation of events. For example, human beings are prone to 'negativity bias' – the tendency to focus disproportionately on unpleasant stimuli. Again, this makes sense from an evolutionary perspective, as unpleasant events might lead to annihilation, whereas pleasant events probably will not. Early humans who were more alert to danger – those who were able to spot and react quickly to threats from the bushes – were far more likely to pass on their genes.

And yet, for many of us, most of the time, life is not so dreadful: Shelly Gable has estimated that a majority of people in prosperous parts of the world enjoy three times more positive experiences in life than negative ones.[5] But still our minds tend to focus on the problems. The title of a famous psychology paper put this bluntly – 'Bad is stronger than good'.[6] Our minds are inclined to look for the downside in any situation, and we learn faster and more deeply from painful experiences than enjoyable ones.

Negativity bias also means that we tend to interpret potentially difficult situations as more threatening than they are – we imagine the worst-case scenario even when things are likely to turn out fine. We see a coiled rope on the ground and we think it's a snake. We hear the creak of pipes at night and a voice in our head screams: 'Intruder!' From a survival perspective, this sort of reaction serves a useful purpose: it's better to worry today and be alive tomorrow than to be happy today and dead tomorrow. But, ultimately, the cost is more unhappiness. Because we are hard-wired to focus on the things that are not going well – and the things that pose a threat to our survival – we tend to ignore the good things in life. We're so busy worrying about whether we've left the gas on that we don't notice or appreciate the gorgeous sunrise on our walk to work. We feel tension in our gut, rather than a warm glow in our heart that might come from the beautiful view.

Negativity bias has an impact on relationships, too. Super-sensitive to threats to our social status (which in the past could lead to ostracism and even death), we are deeply affected by any perceived criticism or rejection from others. John Gottman has found that there needs to be at least five times as many positive as negative interactions between married couples for the relationship to remain stable.[7] In other words, we need a lot of kindness and love for a relationship to survive the effects of even a small amount of conflict.

Our biases come in other forms, too.[8] There's confirmation bias (clinging to beliefs in the face of conflicting evidence), projection bias (assuming most people think like us) and gambler's fallacy (a belief that future outcomes will be affected by disconnected past events). We are prone to change blindness (the failure to notice unexpected shifts in the environmental field) and implicit egotism (the habit of unconsciously preferring people, places and things that we associate with ourselves).

Each of these biases has its benefits. By following apparently established patterns in our experience and environment, the mind learns shortcuts that save cognitive energy and speed up reactions. When these shortcuts work well, we are able to tackle everyday tasks without much effort (for example, we don't have to relearn how to tie our shoelaces every morning) and we are more fully and quickly protected from threats (we see a bus moving fast towards us in the road and don't need to spend a long time weighing up the pros and cons of stepping off the pavement). But when the world fails to conform to our expectations, we may get into trouble. Confirmation bias means we get stuck with outdated opinions; change blindness means we view the world with outdated maps; and projection bias means we assume others think and feel the same as we do. When we are unaware of how our habits and biases affect our perceptions, we live life on autopilot, the state of waking sleep. We may be able to tie our shoelaces without thinking about it, or automatically avoid an approaching bus, but our mind's experience is no more reliable than a dream. It may seem as if we are noticing everything astutely, but when filtered through the mind's projections, our experience is out of kilter with reality. With negativity bias, life is perceived more often as a nightmare than as a pleasant fantasy. This forms the basis for all kinds of mistaken views, misunderstandings and inappropriate reactions. It's what leads to arguments and wars.

We have our own personal biases, too – our past experiences colour what we think and feel. As the neurologist Oliver Sacks put it: 'When we open our eyes each morning, it is upon a world we have spent a lifetime learning to see.'[9] If we were repeatedly bullied at school, we might feel anxiety about status in an organisational setting. If we've recovered from a life-threatening illness, we might be very sensitive to each new ache or pain. If our childhood family home was repossessed by the bank, we might be fearful of financial uncertainty. Interpretations of past events are stored in the unconscious – where they comprise what is known as implicit memory – ready for automatic retrieval at times of similar stress. To avoid a repetition of what hurt us before, we are primed with negative thoughts and unpleasant body sensations – warning signs that danger is approaching. The more stressful the experience was in the past, the stronger the reaction is likely to be now. Moreover, as soon as we start to feel bad, that feeling itself becomes a source of stress and rumination. The worse we feel, the more we tend to interpret a situation as threatening, and so we feel even worse – it's a vicious spiral downwards, as the grooves in our mind become ever deeper set. Two and a half thousand years ago, the Buddha put it like this: 'Whatever a person frequently thinks and ponders upon, that will become the inclination of their mind.'[10]

There's a story of a man who wanted to hang a painting in his living room.[11] He couldn't find his hammer, so he decided to borrow one from his neighbour. Whistling happily, he was just about to knock on the neighbour's door when a thought popped into his head: I borrowed that guy's ladder last week. He might be getting fed up with me.

This stopped the man in his tracks. Then another thought popped up: I saw him in the street yesterday and he didn't smile at me. Perhaps he *is* annoyed.

Then another thought: That's ridiculous. Who'd get annoyed about someone borrowing a hammer? We're neighbours, after all. It's not exactly difficult for him, is it? I'd lend him my hammer if he needed it. And I know he's got a hammer, because he was banging away with it early in the morning last week. He could have woken up the whole street with that racket. Inconsiderate so-and-so! Right, that does it!

With a scowl, the man banged on his neighbour's front door and without waiting for an answer shouted through the letterbox: You can keep your stupid hammer, you selfish idiot!

Once a negative spiral starts, it's difficult to break free from it. When you think you've been slighted by a friend or colleague, it becomes harder to appreciate – or even notice – the glow of a bright sunny day or the privilege of living in a peaceful society with a comfortable bed to rest in every night. Each time we hear the creaking pipe and imagine a burglar downstairs, we are afflicted by powerful body sensations (pumping heart, churning gut, trembling hands) and worrisome ideas (He's coming to get me!). Nothing untoward may have happened, but our thoughts and feelings lend the experience a threatening tone, and the world seems a grimmer place.

The more we get stressed, the more we're likely to suffer from negativity bias, and the more we're likely to interpret events as threatening. The more pessimistic we are, the more we're likely to feel gloomy. This may explain why people who suffer from depression become increasingly vulnerable over time: after a single episode, the relapse rate is roughly 50 per cent; but if a person suffers three episodes, there is a 90 per cent chance that they will experience another one.[12] Depression, like any other experience, seems to forge grooves in the mind and brain, weighting experience and neural structure in a way that leads to more misery. Our perspective on the world assumes a habitual negative hue. Pessimism and fear become more like traits than states of mind. In these situations, the autopilot becomes a hindrance, not a help. Although triggered by present events, our perceptions and reactions are coloured by biases that formed in the past. It's as if we're standing in a hall of mirrors, in thrall to grotesque projections of the mind.

Biases quickened my own descent into depression. I'd been sharply affected by a number of peer rejections in childhood, and although I found salvation in performing well at school, the vulnerabilities remained. I'm very alert to perceived social ostracism, while dropping from a level of top performance can provoke strong anxiety in my mind and body. I was willing to work hard to maintain self-worth, and was fortunate to fly through my early career, with strong friendships and a sense of status. But the memories lay dormant, and my reactions were extreme when romantic and social rejections came. Unprepared for the painful thoughts and feelings that crowded my mind and body, I no longer felt able to keep up the work or friendships that had bolstered my shaky confidence. The spiral downwards was fast and steep.

Stuck in depression, I was hopelessly lost in the biases, unable to find an objective viewpoint. Unaware that my perspective was strongly subjective, I believed my thoughts. Why wouldn't I? Everything in education and life up to that point had taught me that thoughts, feelings and life events *were* experience. I fully identified with them, so they determined my quality of life and degree of happiness. Yet this was an extremely limited way of living, because it relied on habitually arising thoughts and sensations as the sole arbiters of experience, and as the primary drivers of reactions and behaviours.

By deliberately focusing attention on an object of meditation, such as the breath, over and over again, it's possible to train consciously in directing the mind. Although our thoughts and sensations are still subject to habits and biases, we start to view them from a different, less tangled, perspective. First, we bring attention to the experience of the senses, because the mind tends to get caught up in abstractions of thought, becoming embroiled in future-based fantasies or past-based ruminations. By choosing to attend to the experience of breathing, or other sensory experiences in the body, we begin to free ourselves from the tendency to live in our heads.

By coming back to a gentle focus, again and again, whenever we notice distraction, we cultivate the power of chosen attention, strengthening our capacity to perceive aspects of life that often go unnoticed because the mind isn't used to seeing them. By engaging in this work with an attitude of kindness, we are freed from the compulsive need to struggle for success. We let go of berating the mind for not following intention, and instead recognise that it's simply following patterns set over the course of a human lifetime, in addition to the many lifetimes of ancestors who passed their physiology and psychology on to us. Just knowing that these patterns of mind are part of our human legacy, rather than a personal failing, can serve to lighten the overdeveloped sense of responsibility we feel for them.

Working with – rather than against – the mind, we steer a course between struggling against, running away from and ignoring what's happening. But noticing what's happening right now, with an attitude of compassion, and returning to attention whenever we perceive distraction, the mind comes to know itself in a more friendly way, training itself in a way of working that isn't so enslaved to habits.

Remember, the process of training attention is a bit like flexing muscles in a gym. The weight of mental habit draws attention away, but each time this is noticed and attention returns, the power of focus is strengthened. Over time, just as a muscle in the body grows through the effort of resistance, the tendency of the mind to wander can be used as the resistance to cultivate attention. This is a helpful way to view mind wandering: rather than an obstacle to mindfulness practice – something that is annoying – distraction is a force that can help us strengthen attention. Each time you notice the mind has drifted, you have an opportunity to work the muscle of mindfulness.

If, as William James suggested, 'our experience is what we attend to', then developing the capacity to choose *what* we attend to gives us some power to affect our experience. Rather than being drawn by an unconsciously wandering mind into a whirlpool of negativity, meditation practice allows us to pay attention consciously. It enables us to unhitch from some of the more unhelpful and unpleasant trains of thought that afflict us, meaning we no longer spiral unnecessarily into what seems threatening and fearful, and start to avoid the mood states and body sensations invoked by focusing on the dreadful.

In my longest period of depression, I was stuck in negativity for more than two and a half years. But then I started to practise shifting my attention from the frightening thoughts and into sensations of breathing. Resting with the breath began in the daily practice of meditation, but gradually expanded into times when I wasn't sitting on a cushion. As my ability to focus grew, I was more able to let go of ruminative thinking, which allowed my attention to move to a more peaceful place.

Studies suggest that when people train in meditation, their capacity for attention grows. Practitioners are more alert to visual cues that most people fail to see, their memories improve, and they spot changes in the environmental field that others don't notice. Their minds wander less, and they are less caught up in rumination, because their ability to extricate themselves from the stickiness of thoughts and emotions develops.[13] In meditation, we free the control of our minds from the authority of the drunken monkey. We start to decide *what* to focus on, as well as *how* and *when*. Practising meditation decreases 'cognitive rigidity' – the tendency to get stuck in the same mental patterns time and again.[14] Being less caught up in these patterns enables us to be more creative and flexible when responding to challenge. If our habitual ways of dealing with problems prove unhelpful, cognitive flexibility enables us to change course and try something different.

Neuroscientists have identified a neural network that becomes more active when we are lost in mind wandering, and more passive during meditation. It's known as the 'default mode network' because it is triggered by default, automatically, whenever we are *not* paying attention. This network is busy when we find ourselves ruminating or fantasising, caught up in thoughts about ourselves, and its increased activity is linked to states of depression and anxiety.[15] By contrast, when people practise meditation, activity in the default mode network declines,[16] while sectors of the pre-frontal cortex associated with paying attention and sensory processing become more active, as well as thicker.[17] This occurs as people notice mind wandering, disengage from it, and focus attention on the object of meditation, over and over again.

More experienced meditators are able to make this switch from the default mode to the sensory processing mode more consciously. This suggests that they have become more proficient at focusing and refocusing attention.[18] With practice, they appear to become adept at unhooking the mind from automatic thoughts and sensations, letting them go and deciding to focus on something else instead. This is potentially transformative for well-being. Released from automatic mind wandering, and able to focus attention on an aspect of experience that is less likely to stir up misery or anxiety, we are nudged in the direction of happiness, without changing the external circumstances of our lives.

But in mindfulness practice, we do not *just* learn concentration. We also notice when we are *not* paying attention. Having explicitly set the task of placing the mind's eye on a particular object, it becomes much more obvious when the focus has drifted elsewhere. Although we intended to be with the breath, we often find ourselves stuck in a fantasy, or listening to a noise in the street, or pulled towards a twinge in our leg. At this point, the temptation is to become self-critical, get annoyed, or give up.

But if my mind is distracted, and 'I' know that it is distracted, what part of me knows this? Something else – something other than my thinking mind, some greater aspect of consciousness – must be telling me that my attention has wandered.

This is awareness. Each time the mind wanders, at some point awareness kicks in. We notice that the mind has strayed from the intended focus. For instance, we may suddenly realise: Oh, I'm thinking about the shopping, and I'm supposed to be following the breath. As soon as we have awareness of what's happening, of where our attention actually is, we can decide what to do about it. No longer stuck in an automatic mental groove, we can once again follow the guidance we've been given – acknowledge the wandering of the mind with kindness, then gently return it to the intended focus. In other words, we can continue to practise, until we notice that the mind has strayed again, until the next 'Oh . . .' moment – the next moment of awareness.

It's a remarkably simple process, yet the transformation it can generate is revolutionary, much more so than just training attention. We are opening to the recognition that the mind can be aware of its own activity. There is a part of being human that can watch what's happening, as it's happening. So, although we get caught up in our fantasies, ruminations, pain and stress, we can also *know* that we're caught. With the remarkable capacity for awareness, we can observe that experience. And as soon as we observe our experience, we are no longer enslaved by it. We are able to see from a wider perspective. In a remarkable, Houdini-like manoeuvre, we liberate ourselves from the shackles that have bound us to the events of our lives, simply by recognising what's happening.

Awareness neither clings to nor denies what's happening – it simply knows, openly and with interest. A prince once asked the Buddha: 'What do you and your followers do each day?' The Buddha replied: 'We sit, we walk and we eat.' The prince was bemused: 'Everyone sits, walks and eats, so what makes you so different?' The Buddha answered: 'When we sit, we know we are sitting, when we walk, we know we are walking, and when we eat, we know we are eating.'[19]

Having developed the capacity for conceptual thought as a species, might we now take another leap? Can we uncover the capacity for conscious awareness, so we suffer less from the conceptual processes that enabled us to emerge from a state of animal ignorance? Becoming human seems to have meant evolving from unaware and unconcerned to aware and anxious. Perhaps the next step could be to align with an awareness that can begin to free us from that anxiety, while deepening our ability to live conscious lives. Fortunately, as a species, we're already in touch with enough of this awareness to start taking this next step. And we already have access to effective training programmes in the form of contemplative practices, such as meditation. You can't force awareness – it comes as a gift. But by choosing to pay attention, again and again and again, that gift arrives.

Things really began to change for me the moment I 'observed my experience' on that bus ride to Battersea, back in 2001. Whereas my life up to then had been lived on autopilot, for the first time I was able to watch the events in my world – both within me and around me – from a more spacious perspective. Like most of us, I knew how to think and take action, but my thoughts and actions were still being driven automatically – there was little or no awareness of my habitual frames of reference, or of the forces that shaped my way of life. When automatic thinking and reacting failed to sort out my problems, indeed when these thoughts and reactions were part of what made me feel depressed, trying to think and act my way out just tightened the knots of despair, deepening my depression.

Depressive rumination isn't a good strategy for resolving the problem of depressive rumination. But fighting or trying to change the thoughts was just as futile. Buttressed by the force of habit, not only did the thoughts not listen to my commands, but I was quickly frustrated by my powerlessness to control my own mind. The more I struggled, zeroing in on problems with impotent rage, the more trapped I became. Meditation practice helped me to understand that I approached everything in life through the filter of thought, and mostly negative thought at that. With practice, the moments of spacious awareness – the 'Oh . . .' moments when I noticed the mind wandering – became more frequent and sustained.

Seeing with awareness changes everything. As soon as we notice thinking, we're no longer lost *in* thought. In a moment of awareness, we are freed from identification with ideas. Thoughts still happen, of course, and they may be as distorted as ever. But if we can be open to seeing thoughts from awareness, it doesn't matter if a lot of them are happening, if they seem out of control, or if they are more worrisome or negative than we'd like them to be. With awareness, we can recognise them as just aspects of the mind's activity, rather than be compelled to believe that thoughts are who we are, or try to ignore or banish them.

This is so empowering because, as we have seen, thinking is riddled with bias. As soon as we see thought as nothing more than thought – mental events arising in awareness rather than as *me* or *my* thoughts – we free ourselves from the tangle of thinking.

Our relationship with the rest of experience changes, too. Sensations in the body become just sensations – arising, changing, then fading, moment by moment. When we are in pain, we notice the uncomfortable feelings, and notice as attention is drawn to them, but in awareness they can be experienced not so much as *my* pain – and automatically identified with – but more as mere sensations that occur within the body. We don't have to buy into the thoughts that typically accompany discomfort – such as 'Why can't I stop this from happening?' or 'How long is this going to last?' – so we're less likely to react to them with frustration or rage. Instead, by seeing what's happening from a place of awareness – sensations and thoughts arising, passing through, dissolving – we are less caught up in what's happening.

According to research conducted by Jennifer Daubenmier, experiencing thoughts and emotions with mindful awareness – rather than with identification and judgement – provides a buffer against the stressful effect they can otherwise have on the body. People with high levels of mindfulness have lower levels of cortisol, even when they experience anxiety, low mood or ruminative thoughts.[20]

Experience can be unpleasant, and sometimes there is nothing we can do about that. We might lose our job, overhear an unkind remark, get burgled, be diagnosed with cancer, suffer a flat tyre on the motorway – all kinds of major and minor losses and insults are visited on each of us over the course of a lifetime. If we fully identify with such experiences as *my* misfortunes, and treat the habitually arising thoughts, emotions and sensations that accompany them as the sum total of *my* experience, we are doomed to stress and liable to react in ways that serve only to exacerbate it.

Perceiving with awareness doesn't eliminate these troubles, or stop some experiences from being unpleasant, or remove the bias from our thoughts about them. But it *does* enable them to be experienced quite differently. It leads to greater equanimity, which in turn reduces both painful attachment and the likelihood of unconscious, impulsive or unbalanced reactions.

How meditation trains attention and awareness

In mindfulness practice, we gently work the muscle of attention. By placing our focus on a chosen object, we cultivate the capacity to direct the mind more consciously. By patiently coming back to that object when we notice attention has wandered, the mind is trained to settle into stillness. With time, practice and an attitude of friendliness, the mind can become less wild and speedy, more workable and more responsive.

The difficulty of sustaining attention on a single object demonstrates how we tend to get caught in grasping, aversion or distraction. By choosing not to give attentional energy to our urges to rush, run or avoid, and instead coming back to centre the mind on the breath, body or some other chosen place, we are able to see the automatic habits of the mind from a new perspective. We become aware of them, rather than caught up in them. This act of noticing is transformational, because it means we are no longer unconsciously trapped in the patterns that ensnare us. We realise that that the problem is not our thoughts, feelings and impulses but our identification with them.

As soon as we learn to notice experience moment by moment, we start to free ourselves from blindly following our old habits. We may not need to do more than watch and let be. We start to become, as Ram Dass put it, 'connoisseurs of our neuroses' – knowing them so well that we are no longer in thrall to them. It's a bit like having the radio on in the background – the same tunes play over and over again, but we don't have to sing along. As we become increasingly familiar with the pull of our thoughts and impulses, we can gently practise unhooking from them, just by recognising them.

Practice to try: Mindfulness of breath, body, sounds and thoughts

This practice begins with the breath as an anchor for attention, before expanding the focus into the whole body. By focusing on sounds, we see how phenomena are habitually received and processed in our minds and learn to see the concepts and reactions that get overlaid onto basic experience. Finally, by looking at the process of thinking directly, we reverse our usual pattern of being caught up in it. Instead, we observe thoughts as they appear, pass through and dissolve in the mindstream.

1. Settle into a good posture for sitting meditation – soles of the feet on the ground, sitting on a firm seat with the upper body upright. Hold the body in a way that invokes a sense of confidence, softness, openness and dignity.

2. Practise mindfulness of breathing for a time. Invite attention into the sensations of breathing, letting the rise and fall of the breath be experienced. When you notice the mind wandering, be interested in what has distracted attention from the breath, acknowledging it gently before shepherding attention back to the breathing.

3. After a period of mindful breathing, perhaps five to ten minutes, let attention open up and expand to the whole body. Let all of your body sensations be experienced, fully present to the waxing and waning of feeling, wherever you notice them in the body. With the mind, ride the waves of sensation. When you notice the mind has wandered, maybe into thinking, first congratulate yourself on this moment of

awareness, then patiently bring attention back to the body again.

4. After a period of practising mindfulness of body, turn your attention to sounds. Imagine that your ears are like microphones, picking up sounds, registering them just as they are, as vibrations. Notice pitch, tone and volume, staying present to the ongoing fluctuations as the soundscape changes from moment to moment. As you attend to the bare sensations of sounds, you will probably find concepts and other sensations happening alongside – thoughts will name the sounds or categorise them into types. Other thoughts may appear as memories, associations or judgements. See if you can allow all of these to pass through in the background of awareness as you offer attention to the sounds, uncoupled from the thoughts that accompany them. Similarly, if sounds trigger body sensations – perhaps relaxation or tensing – is it possible to allow these to happen without grasping or pushing them away? As best you can, stay with the sounds and allow everything else to play out in the background.

5. Finally, bring mindfulness to thoughts. Perhaps imagine yourself sitting down in the theatre of the mind and watching your thoughts appear as a monologue or a dialogue (or maybe as a vast chorus of voices). The task – not easy – is to stay in your seat while the voices shout, cajole, whisper, fall silent, disappear or demand your attention, without being seduced into believing they are facts, rather than just thoughts. Keep watching the show, allowing any sensations to be experienced in awareness, without following or resisting them (and coming back with kindness when you notice you *have* followed or resisted).

Similarly, when you suddenly realise you have wandered on stage as an actor in the play, attached to a thought rather than being its observer, just acknowledge this, perhaps with a smile, then return to your observer's seat. Remember, each time you untangle from a thought with awareness, you strengthen the muscle of mindfulness, and are cultivating the capacity to notice thoughts, rather than being driven unconsciously by concept.

CHAPTER FIVE

Where Everything that is, is Welcome

Peace is this moment without judgement.
This moment in the heart-space where
everything that is, is welcome.

Dorothy Hunt[1]

There's a tale told of the Tibetan yogi Milarepa, whose meditation cave was overrun with demons. When he first finds the
demons in his cave, Milarepa starts chasing them round furiously,
lashing out with blows in a desperate attempt to make them leave.
But no matter how hard he fights or how fast he runs, the demons
stay put; indeed, they seem rather to enjoy the sport. Finally
exhausted from his efforts, Milarepa has what he thinks is a great
idea. He'll teach the demons to meditate! Surely, when they've
learned the benefits of mindfulness, they'll thank him and be on
their way. Pleased with himself and his generous, ingenious plan,
he invites the demons to sit down and starts giving instruction on
how to be mindful, expounding key points of a Buddhist way of life.
Are the demons impressed? Not a bit of it – they just stare at him
blankly, bug-eyed and bemused.

Realising his plan is not so clever after all, Milarepa dries up, then gives up. He shrugs his shoulders and sighs: 'Okay, demons, you win. Welcome to my cave, make yourselves at home. Now, what can *you* teach *me*?' At these words, the demons dissolve into space. Aside, that is, from one particularly menacing creature, who glowers at the yogi with a fierce and hungry look. 'Right, scary demon,' says an emboldened Milarepa, walking towards the monster and placing his head in its mouth. 'You want to have me for dinner? It looks like I can't stop you, so go ahead and eat!' The last demon evaporates, too.

When I first heard this story, in the early days of my practice, I didn't understand it. I thought teaching the demons to meditate was indeed an ingenious and generous idea, so why didn't it work? And as for putting your head in a demon's mouth ... well, why would anyone do that, even if there was no chance of escape? None of it made any sense.

Similar confusion arose when I was halfway through the MBCT course. In the fifth session, we were invited to practise 'turning towards difficulty'. This means bringing a gentle focus towards whatever is troubling or uncomfortable at that moment. This wasn't the first time I'd heard these instructions, but I was so used to meditating on the breath, allowing everything else to pass by in the background, that I rarely attempted this other approach. In the MBCT session, when invited to focus on the difficult, I just carried on attending to my breathing. We were asked to discuss the practice afterwards in pairs, and I explained my decision to my partner: 'I know I can ride out unpleasant events over time by bringing my mind back to the breath. So why give them more focus than they need? Won't turning towards them make them seem worse than they are?'

The question kept coming back to me. If turning towards difficulty wasn't helpful, then why was it taught as a practice on this course, which had an impressive record in reducing depression?

And why was it often taught at Buddhist centres, often through stories such as Milarepa and the demons? Perhaps I could learn something from my reluctance to try it. What could this tell me about how I reacted to problems in life when I wasn't meditating? And what would happen if I responded to depression not by turning to the breath and hoping the pain away, but by breathing *into* the unwanted sensations?

  This was a pivotal point in my practice. As I became more famil-iar with mindfulness-based approaches to stress, depression and pain, I realised that two key instructions were often emphasised, and that I'd mostly managed to avoid both of them ever since I'd started. The first was bringing mindfulness to the whole body, as in the body scan. The second was turning towards difficulty – a deliberate decision to open oneself to what was scary, stressful and unpleasant. I had learned a lot by practising and studying the principles of Buddhism, but this way of being wasn't steadily embodied, probably because my pattern is to be heady and evasive. At my core, I still thought difficult thoughts and feelings should just disappear. Hence, I hung on to the breath until they did so, or immersed myself in reading about practice to distract myself from stressful sensations. The clear focus and structure of an eight-week mindfulness course directly challenged those tenden-cies, drawing my attention back to my body – and to what was difficult – again and again. Gradually, over time and with practice, this led to a much deeper shift in how I manage problems, and a much healthier relationship with the symptoms that I used to call 'depression'.

Through daily meditation, extended retreats and a lot of reading, I had developed an awareness of the patterns that led to anxiety and depression. I saw how I fell into despair when vulnerable points in my psyche were pressed; and I came to understand that my reactions were biased. But bare attention can take us only part of the way along the path of mindfulness. Notwithstanding all the practice and study, I still had a fractious relationship with difficult experiences. Whenever strong unpleasant feelings and thoughts arose, the best I could manage was to breathe, watch and wait while fear, rage and shame moved through me like storm clouds. Of course, this was a lot better than it had been in the days before meditation, when I had tried to wrestle with this internal weather or blow it away. But there was still something quietly passive – and subtly resistant – about my reactions. When I felt uncomfortable, my attitude to practice was not peaceful – it carried a sense of annoyance and disappointment.

Why did this keep happening? Why couldn't I continue to feel well for very long? Surely, if I could just practise for long enough, hard enough, in the right way, the pattern of suffering should stop. The problem was that I was trying to bargain with the demons of depression, trying to persuade them to leave through meditation. Practice was supposed to bring a positive result – follow the instructions and the demons will disappear. I couldn't understand Milarepa's error in trying to teach his demons to meditate, because I had adopted precisely the same approach to deal with mine. Inevitably, the result was much the same – an uneasy stand-off. Some days I felt okay, but on others I felt overwhelmed, no matter how much I meditated. On those days, I would want to be happy, but I actually felt angry, fearful and withdrawn. I found it impossible to accept that things were not going as well as I would have hoped, so I ramped up the resistance to what was happening. And that definitely didn't feel okay.

I was caught in a state of conditional mindfulness: I'm happy to meditate, but you must give me what I want. Secretly, I'd hope for some of those amazing experiences I'd had at Dechen Choling, when the world was a shimmering kaleidoscope of colour. Of course, in trying to force an experience of feeling good – and eliminate feeling bad – I was perpetuating the same old patterns of craving and aversion that practice invites us to abandon. I might have stopped trying to chase my demons, but I hadn't yet made peace with them. I was running from the circumstances, thoughts and sensations that made up my reality. By hoping that mindfulness of breathing would bring about perpetual happiness and calm, and then by focusing tightly on that, I was subtly pushing everything that wasn't pleasant in my mind, body and life into the background. Another of Atisha's mind-training aphorisms warns: 'Don't turn gods into demons.' I was doing that whenever I tried to meditate in order to escape from life's difficulties. I was turning something useful into yet another demon. Meditation was helping me to cope, to a degree, but it was a partial form of practice and it brought only partial rewards.

This meant that I still tended to get caught in the loop of depression whenever stressful situations arose. Railing against my own feelings, these became more stresses to fight, sometimes long after the trigger that caused them had passed. Thus, the battle with depression itself perpetuated my misery. Ironically, by anxiously resisting difficult feelings and thoughts, I kept them going. Because of my meditation practice, I had some understanding that this was happening, but I still seemed unable to change the pattern.

Sigmund Freud once said that giving insight to a psychotherapy patient was like offering a menu to a starving man. Sometimes I felt like that starving man – I was more aware of my patterns, but frustrated by not being able to drop them. Mindfulness of breathing helped to an extent, as it offered some sanctuary from the storms; and the shift in perspective that came from awareness helped to loosen depression's grip. But a fuller transformation eluded me. I had become stuck on the breath as a place of anchor, not aware that the practice went further than breathing as distraction and reassurance. I had reached a point where I could read the menu, but I couldn't eat the meal.

Difficulties are unavoidable. We may elude or mask them for a time, but suffering is an integral part of being alive – from birth to death, and through everything in between, we encounter dissatisfaction of all kinds. Physical pain, loss, grief, anxiety, low mood, automatic negative thoughts, sadness, anger, being blamed or hurt by others, a change from fortunate to unfortunate circumstances, ageing, and knowing that we will die one day are just a few of the inevitable insults that life throws at us. And there's nothing we can do to prevent them – whether external events or inner thoughts and feelings, much of what happens to us is impervious to conscious choice. We don't decide to feel sick, tired, sad, anxious or depressed, just as we don't choose where we are born, how tall we grow, when a lover leaves us, or whether a storm hits our house. Of course, circumstances lead up to these events, and we may have influence over parts of them – we may be able to alter some of what comes later by adjusting our reaction to any given situation. But once an event is happening – both the change in circumstance and the thought or feeling that accompanies it – there's nothing we can do to stop it. What is already here *is* already here.

Humans have evolved to meet difficulty with attack or aversion. Something we don't like arrives and we instinctively want to get rid of it. This is a natural reaction. After all, why would anyone *want* pain or stress? It is hard-wired into us – human ancestors who were successful at slipping away from predators were more likely to survive and pass on their genes. So we follow the habits that benefited our forebears by moving fast to remove (or remove ourselves from) any threat to our well-being. Whether it's a hungry lion, a poisonous snake, an oncoming bus or an angry neighbour, we are strongly impelled to get away as quickly as possible.

Our bodies are geared to make this happen. On hearing a rustle in the grass, human beings jump automatically. The heart beats faster, pumping blood to the muscles, which are instantly ready to start running. This is accompanied by more activity in the amygdala, the brain's almond-shaped 'alert centre', which sits at the apex of the limbic system. Stress hormones course through the body. These generate anxiety – a sudden churning in the belly, tension in the legs and arms, tightening neck muscles – as the head turns instinctively to the location of the sound. Unbidden thoughts arise: What was that? A snake? All of these reactions happen below the level of conscious choice. This should come as no surprise, because hanging around on the savannah, waiting to become a lion's lunch, is not a good survival plan.

Unfortunately, though, we experience the same automatic reactions when we face very different threats. Operating on the principle of 'If it might be a lion, we had better react as if it surely is', our bodies are wired for survival, not happiness. If you miss one hungry lion creeping up behind you, you won't make it past lunchtime. On the other hand, if you mistake five hundred rustles of the wind in the grass for a hungry predator, you will endure the unnecessary panic of your heart jumping into your throat five hundred times, but you'll also have a head start when the lion really is behind you, When the danger is real, you might just make it through to tomorrow.

But what we perceive as dangerous now has much more to do with human relationships. Most of us don't come face to face with lions these days – we are far more likely to feel spooked by angry neighbours, the rejection of loved ones, or a deluge of emails from colleagues or clients. Historically, because ostracism from a social group greatly increased our ancestors' vulnerability to attack, our bodies' systems respond to difficult human interactions in much the same way as they respond to spotting a hungry lion in the bushes. So, while overhearing a sly insult may not be life-threatening, our bodies do not differentiate between the slight and a prowling predator. *Any* situation that is perceived as a threat can lead to heart palpitations, sweaty palms and nausea. In addition to feeling unpleasant, this can drive us into automatic actions. We might feel tense, angry and panicky – and determined to resolve the problem in one way or another. The body's systems provide two main options: flee (perhaps run away and hide in the bathroom) or attack (shout a curt retort across the office or even square up to the person who issued the insult). Sensations in our bodies trigger fast, unthinking, habitual reactions that might be appropriate when facing a wild animal's assault on the savannah, but which are far less helpful when dealing with a condescending colleague in an office. Running away from that colleague will do little to diminish the perceived threat of ostracism, and nor will responding aggressively. Both reactions will merely ramp up the stress and provoke an even stronger impulse to run or attack in the future. Of course, this is just an annoying colleague, but the body's stress reaction system doesn't know that. Working on an intuitive rather than a logical level, the primitive system reacts on the assumption that the danger could be mortal.

Many of the problems we face today are chronic – email pile-ups, relationship difficulties, illness and pain – and they will not be solved by running away from or battling against them. Aggressive or evasive reactions almost always make the situation worse, because they entail trying to get rid of or away from a problem that cannot be destroyed or dodged. The more the stress persists, the longer the stress reaction continues, and the worse we feel. Developed as a short-term emergency reaction to *acute* threats, prolonged activation of the stress reaction system not only makes us feel more stressed but predisposes us to a range of undesirable mental and physical health effects, such as anxiety and depression, diminished immune system function, sleep disorders, irritability, low energy, poor concentration and high blood pressure.[2] It's a vicious cycle – the more stressed we feel, the worse things seem, and the worse things seem, the more stressed we feel.

And even that's not the end of the problem. As we explored in the previous chapter, human beings have developed the capacity to reflect on experience. This means that we can learn lessons from the past and imagine the future, but it also means that we tend to ruminate, blame and worry. When symptoms of stress persist, the thinking mind often jumps in and tries to work out what is happening. Of course, we don't want to feel stressed, and we know that our symptoms are making us unhappy. The analytical mind, which is usually so good at identifying problems and searching for solutions, starts to whirr away: 'I feel terrible. Why can't I snap out of this? I should be able to do *something*. This is stupid. It's illogical. I must be able to sort it out.'

But, in trying to help, the analytical mind just makes everything worse, because our stress reaction systems – as well as our moods and body sensations more generally – are not controlled by the more recently evolved logical, thinking mind. We are unable to *choose* not to feel stressed simply because we realise that stress isn't helpful. Body sensations and mood states may change over time, and they may be influenced by events, attitudes or actions, but they do not respond to the instant demands of thinking. So the self-conscious instruction to stop feeling sad/angry/in pain/ stressed may result in us feeling *worse*, because it invites us to elevate our resistance to what's going on, which in turn increases our frustration when the resistance fails to stop the unpleasant experience.

And so the vicious cycle deepens: unpleasant experience leads to stress reaction, which leads to rumination, which leads to aversion, which leads to more unpleasant experience, which leads to greater stress reaction, which leads to more rumination, which leads to even more aversion, and so on. Struggling with an experience that cannot be changed in the moment – be it pain, low mood or automatic negative thoughts – is counter-productive because it exacerbates stress and creates even more unpleasant thoughts and sensations. Daniel Wegner calls these 'ironic processes'[3] – by trying to get rid of an unpleasant experience, we make it worse. This isn't exactly a hole of our own making – the stressors we face are real and there may be nothing we can do to stop them – but by reacting in this way we are certainly taking a spade and digging further down.

We can untangle from this pattern by getting to know it, and mindfulness helps us to bring habits to consciousness. By pausing to watch what's happening, we deprive the reaction itself of energy. When observing rather than identifying with what's happening, we no longer ramp up stress with our attitude and actions.

Once we are more able to see our patterns, we can try something different. But what? We know that trying to eliminate pain and stress doesn't work, so what about something more radical? What about turning towards it? We *are* already practising this to some extent when we bring mindfulness to breathing. Every time we come back to the breath, we are moving closer to the experience of our bodies, where all of our feelings are felt. By anchoring the mind to this moment of breath, we are beginning to stay present to the body, countering the habit of zooming off into thinking. The breath is always in the here and now – like all other sensations, it can be felt only in the present moment. For instance, while you can *think* about yesterday's breath, or tomorrow's breath, you cannot *feel* it. Mindful breathing thus brings us back into the experience of reality, drawing us back from flights of fancy.

It also encourages the body to enter into its 'rest and recuperate' mode – after escaping from a predator, an animal may spend some time in a quiet space, gradually slowing its breathing, as its body systems drop back into balance and the stress reaction dissipates. The stillness and steadiness of meditation may help to trigger this by reminding the body to relax a little. Telling yourself to calm down doesn't usually help, but you may be able to invite calm by letting go into breathing. However, we cannot rely on the breath to bring total relief – the power of perceived threat is generally stronger than the power of meditation as a calming influence. In the past, this was good news because our ancestors would have been much easier targets for lions if they had sat still and focused on their breathing. The body cannot be fooled into relaxation if apparent threats continue to lurk.

All of our impulses and logic tell us that seeking out pain is madness. And they're right, of course, if we are contemplating putting our hands on a burning stove or walking in front of a bus. But these same powerful survival instincts become counter-productive when they are linked to automatically arising thoughts, emotions and body sensations, when the perception of threat is precisely that – a perception, not reality. Fortunately, because we are partly conscious beings – and do not function entirely on autopilot – we can respond differently, in so far as we have the mental tools to notice what's happening and react accordingly.

Transformation comes with a shift in our relationship with what's going on. If we can meet what's happening with an attitude of acceptance and allow, or even welcome, what's here with friendliness, then a new signal is sent to the mind and body. This means making a confident, embodied assertion that everything is okay at a basic level, and that we believe we are capable of managing what's here for as long as it's here. Of course, this is far easier said than done, because it flies in the face of millions of years of evolution. But it is feasible. The work begins when we practise staying present to our felt experience, rather than distracting from it, and patiently coming back when we notice the mind has wandered. And it progresses as we gently move towards whatever we find without reservation or expectation. Because this method goes against all of our inherent conditioning, because it contradicts all of our default reactions (aggression, rumination, distraction and escape), because it doesn't seem to make any intuitive sense, it cannot be simply magicked into being. Forging this groove in the psyche demands repetition, repetition and more repetition.

Fortunately, that is the essence of meditation – a repeated experience of skilful working with difficulty. First, we learn to stop and be still, rather than automatically react on impulse. We slow things down. We also learn how to direct attention. We notice how the mind is habitually drawn from a chosen focus, often to painful thoughts and sensations, and learn how to bring it back (albeit fleetingly at first). We keep practising, and every time we notice the wandering of the mind, and return it to the breath, we uncouple our identity from thoughts and sensations that urge us to react.

We also practise attending to the body, which can have a steadying effect. All sorts of body sensations occur – both pleasant and unpleasant – but we practise not reacting to any of them. We just feel, watch and keep coming back to the sensations themselves as the focal points for gentle attention. We invite a sense of groundedness by feeling our contact with the earth – feet on the ground, bottom on the chair if we're sitting, or back on the floor in a body scan. We breathe with the body and keep coming back to presence, whether we feel elated, bored, joyful, depressed, fearful, confident, angry or tired. We let go of the struggle to escape from the body when it is in pain, and we stop trying to force more pleasant sensations. Instead, we just gently work with what is, while it is. Present to the body, coming back to it time and again, we start to counter the 'fight or flight' habit.

If we feel discomfort as we practise, we notice it, become curious about it, let it be felt. Dropping the struggle with things as they are can help to diminish the sense of stress in our minds and bodies, as we practise treating our experience as less of a threat. Instead, we meet it as we might a friend – with a sense of trust, interest and openness. Noticing and feeling what's happening from a place of present-centred curiosity, we no longer try to distract from or resist what's already happening. Rumination and struggle fade away as we offer our attention to the arising, changing and ebbing of sensation, moment by moment. Stress is released, paradoxically, when we no longer try to escape from it.

Ingrained habit tells us that peace can be attained only through struggle. But true peace is the absence of struggle. So, instead of futile attempts to push, pull or analyse our way out of difficulty, we let ourselves experience it, moving our attention into it. When we are willing to let the moment be as it is, the battle created by our frantic resistance starts to ease. We stop chasing demons, stop trying to change them, and start to get to know them.

However, as the story of Milarepa and his demons illustrates, we can go one step further. Once we are familiar with staying present to sensation through our practice, we can begin to experiment with deliberately moving our attention *towards* troubling inner experience. This means consciously directing our mind into feelings that are difficult for us to bear. There might be physical discomfort, such as aches, pains or itches. Or there could be emotional distress – a feeling of sadness, anger or boredom, perhaps. These emotions will likely have physical manifestations, too – churning, tightness, heat, pressure, shakiness – and specific locations where we feel them most, such as in the stomach, legs, head or chest. Like Milarepa, we offer our bodies up to the demons.

When turning towards difficulty, we experience sensations that are uncoupled from the thoughts that usually accompany them. We stay with the sensations and breathe with them, letting the breath be an anchor to help us be present to whatever we are finding. We might also practise breathing *into* them, riding with the sensations of discomfort, just as we ride the feeling of the breath moving into and out of the body. Moving into sensations deliberately and directly, our attention can unhook from the urge to pull away from the difficult feelings, or to try to resolve them, or to get wound up by them. As we decide simply to let them be, we find that they are more likely to let us be, too. When we let go of resisting them, their power to control us fades.

Untangled from thoughts and reactions, which we know aren't always accurately or proportionately weighted to the events that trigger them, we can look into the experience of difficulty with a more courageous, centred presence. We alter the experience by noticing its constituent aspects and relating to them with gentle connection, rather than the desperate lunges or swerves that heighten stress. Difficulties are sometimes *dissolved* rather than *resolved*, and acceptance is the paradoxical alchemy that produces change.

The core learnings of a mindfulness course are working in tandem here. By noticing what is happening, we observe our getting caught in difficulty as well as our desire to avoid it, or solve it by thinking or doing. By staying present and bringing attention *to* the difficulty, we develop a profoundly different relationship with it. Gently undoing the usual patterns of grasping pleasure and avoiding pain, these often frantic and futile reactions are given no energy. Instead, through our compassionate, courageous abiding, we offer an antidote to stressful habit energy. We train in returning again and again to confident presence, allowing ourselves to *feel* rather than always leaping to thought or reaction.

Gentleness is a vital element in this approach. It's easy to become frustrated with our minds and bodies for not working as we might hope. Many of us have been trained to learn by pushing, rushing, goading ourselves into change. But when we relate to our experience with harsh judgement or hard pushing, we undermine our mindfulness, because these mindsets are laced with aggression, and a resistance to reality. Instead, by tenderly noticing and allowing ourselves to feel discomfort, we begin to escape from the stress of striving.

An eager Zen student once asked his teacher: 'How long will it take me to reach enlightenment, if I practise diligently?'

'Ten years,' replied his teacher, with a smile.

'That's not quick enough,' wailed the student. 'What if I am really determined, practising harder than anyone you've ever known? How long will it take then?'

'Twenty years,' said the teacher.

When our practice is fused with equanimity, compassion, curiosity and steadfastness, rather than any ambition to attain a goal, the benefits of mindfulness are likely to appear. We don't have to force these attitudes – their cultivation is built into the practice.

Turning towards difficulty is challenging enough even when we feel strong. I wouldn't recommend it to a novice meditator, or someone in a lot of physical or emotional pain, unless they have the guidance of an experienced teacher. If you are overwhelmed by suffering, it may be advisable to postpone learning to meditate, or at least to begin very gently. My first teacher was very wise to start me off with mindful tea-drinking, and then gradually introduce a sitting practice – for only a few minutes at a time – over several months.

Of course, I abandoned this gentle approach by leaping into extended retreats, and then becoming a permanent resident at a meditation centre. With hindsight, I now realise that my emotional explosions at Dechen Choling were probably due in part to a heightened awareness of feeling, generated by intensive meditation, at a point when I lacked the understanding or steadiness to stay with the experience. But I don't regret the path I chose, because those outbursts of emotion contributed to my shift from a habit of trying to suppress feelings, or force them to change, and to the beginnings of acceptance. My top had begun to blow anyway, in the years before I began to meditate. The intensive practice just lifted the lid quicker, perhaps before I knew how to handle what gushed out. This made for quite a rollercoaster ride, and perhaps my reluctance to turn towards difficulty was a sensible safety mechanism. Perhaps I didn't yet have the resources to cope with what was coming up, until I'd stayed with the breath for a few more years.

After I returned to England, my practice was more firmly anchored, and I wasn't so blown about by the storms of emotion. Eventually, I was ready to put my head in the demon's mouth. When I first tried turning towards difficulty, the urge to pull away was strong. I didn't want to experience pain more intimately. I held on to a residual belief that I could lessen the stress by dis-tracting from or battling against the feeling. But gradually, over time, whenever the symptoms of stress arose, I tested the water and swam towards them. In meditation, I would move my mind into my body, focusing gentle attention within – wherever I felt intense sensation. When I wasn't practising formally, I would bring my mind back to the body, as often as I remembered. Sometimes I'd practise this for no more than a few seconds before either the autopilot kicked in and catapulted my mind elsewhere, or I decided that I'd done enough and that the gentlest and most sensible action was now to take a break.

Over time, I've worked with this practice more and more. I return to a place of mind–body union, remembering myself into alignment, whenever stress stretches me out of balance. When the old anxiety symptoms come, I feel them at first, perhaps as much as ever. My body reverts to feeling crunched and jittery, and my mind is crowded with negative thoughts, just as it was in the old, dark days. But my relationship with them is quite different now. I suspect I notice these symptoms earlier than I used to – I think I used to be oblivious to the signs of stress until they had overwhelmed me. Also, instead of getting automatically freaked out by what I'm feeling, I'm more able to breathe with it, be with it, tune into it, turn into it. Doom-laden thoughts chunter on, and while I offer them interest, I don't believe what they say. I know they are tainted with negative bias.

Gently giving attention to the heart palpitations, the pressure in my nose and chest, the ripple of worry in my gut, I signal to my body that I will not be fighting or fleeing from the supposed threat to my welfare; nor do I treat the unpleasant sensations as a problem. Holding them gently in awareness, to the best of my ability, I carry on with the day, perhaps with an extra promise to practise steadiness and kindness. This gives another signal that what's happening does not have to overwhelm me. I remind myself that it's okay to feel like this, that I can't make the experience go away immediately, but that if I practise a gentle, kind, confident and steady relationship with it, I will give myself the best chance of managing it well, while it lasts.

The results, over time, have been remarkable. In addition to reducing the length of time that each episode lasts, this approach has shifted my perception of what depression is. The more I practise moving towards difficulty – approaching painful thoughts and sensations with friendliness – the less they seem to bother me. And as their impact on my life reduces, can I really call this depression any more? After all, surely the label implies an unwanted experience from which sufferers are desperate to escape? Yet here I am, accepting the experience much as I would a common cold – it's not particularly pleasant, but nor is it a reason for panic. I've even invented a new word to describe it – 'blurgy' – which I think captures the sense of an unfortunate, passing malady that responds well to patience, rather than to rage and resistance. I now believe that part of my 'depression' comprised resistance to the anxious feelings and thoughts that came with difficulty – a habitual reaction that turned up the volume on any suffering. By learning not to buy into those reactions, and by not fuelling them, I started to change my pattern of experience. By putting my head in the demon's mouth, the demon is dissolving.

Or at least it's no longer a demon. Difficulties haven't vanished. Unpleasant sensations and thoughts still come, but when I make them my friends, they no longer bother me nearly as much as they once did. Making them my enemies gave them the power to floor me. Sometimes I forget this, and they transform back into demons for a while. But I just have to remember to make friends with them again, and I am more able to cope.

The science of staying present

Research into mindfulness has shown the benefits of staying present, and of gently turning towards difficulty. Mindfulness-based relapse prevention (MBRP) trains people with addictive habits to manage their cravings mindfully by staying present to the sensations of craving, rather than trying to distract from them, avoid them or defeat them. In a large trial of MBRP, mindfulness-trained patients drank alcohol and used drugs significantly less than those who were treated with cognitive-behavioural approaches, and a control group who attended twelve-step and psycho-education groups. The authors of the study conclude that mindfulness was the most successful approach, especially over the longer term, because it enabled patients to 'monitor and skilfully cope with discomfort associated with craving or negative effect'.[4] A similar study with smokers found that mindfulness training was more than five times as effective as a standard smoking cessation programme, as measured by abstinence from cigarettes after four months (31 per cent compared to 6 per cent).[5] Another study has suggested that mindful people are more able to tolerate their own distress, rather than react in harmful ways.[6]

There are benefits to staying present with physical, as well as emotional, discomfort. Fadel Zeidan and colleagues suggest that meditation practice is associated with brain changes that indicate and reflect shifts in people's experience of, and relationship with, pain.[7] Meditators show decreased activity in the primary somatosensory cortex (an area of the brain involved in registering pain) and increased activity in three areas involved in the regulation of pain – the anterior insula, the anterior cingulate cortex and the pre-frontal cortex. When gently turning towards pain, people report that they experience less of it, and their resistance usually decreases. They may not get so caught up in the negative stories and evasive reactions that tend to accompany pain but do nothing to stop it (and which, indeed, may increase the mind's perception of it). This may be why people with chronic conditions

have reported reductions in pain after training
in mindfulness, even though they still have their
illness.[8]

As far back as 1971, Robert Wallace and Herbert
Benson found that meditation reduced activity in
the sympathetic nervous system,[9] which controls the
'fight or flight' reaction. More recently, attending a
mindfulness course has been shown to reduce activity
and grey matter volume in the amygdala – a key
indicator of how strongly this reaction is triggered.
With mindfulness training also comes a thickening
in parts of the pre-frontal cortex – the region directly
behind the forehead – which may be connected to
a strengthening of the body's capacity to regulate
stress.[10] Connections between the amygdala and
other parts of the brain weaken after mindfulness
training.[11]

One part of the pre-frontal cortex associated with
stress regulation is the anterior cingulate cortex
(ACC). Poor ACC function tends to correlate with
impulsive behaviour and mental inflexibility – which
are both common among people who are under stress.
Experienced meditators display more activity in the
ACC, and better stress regulation. The capacity to self-
manage during difficult situations may be trainable
at a very young age. One study that tracked a group
of pre-school children who attended a mindfulness
programme over six months found that they were
less impulsive (more able to regulate) than a group of
children who did not receive the training.[12]

Just the act of describing unpleasant experiences mindfully can have a positive effect on stress levels. In one study, people with a fear of spiders were asked to walk towards and try to touch a live tarantula. Some were invited to reassure themselves as they approached the spider, while others were advised to distract themselves from what they were trying to do. A third group was encouraged to acknowledge and turn towards their fear, saying something like: 'I am frightened by the big ugly spider.' The members of this third group – those who openly stayed present to their fear – got closest to the tarantula, felt least upset by the experience, and had the least sweaty palms.[13]

Staying present to difficulties seems to have a significant impact on well-being. In Matt Killingsworth's studies of wandering minds, he has found that people are less happy when their minds are distracted, even when they are engaged in an activity that we would usually describe as unpleasant. So, for instance, even though most people are not keen on commuting, they tend to be happier if their minds turn towards the experience of the journey rather than wander away from it.[14] Other studies have suggested that setting oneself the goal of avoiding stress *increases* the long-term risk of depression. By contrast, if we view stress as a normal, helpful indicator – something we can handle and from which we can learn – rather than as something to eliminate, we are more likely to experience good health and emotional well-being.[15]

Practice to try: Turning towards difficulty

When practising mindfulness of breath and body, coming back to focus when the mind wanders, we are already training in presence, irrespective of whether our experience is enjoyable. If you have followed the practices outlined in the previous chapters, you have probably felt some discomfort while meditating – be it a physical pain, a difficult emotion, or an unpleasant thought. By gently returning attention to the breath or the whole body, we are learning to manage these experiences wisely, consciously moving attention to a centred place of steady presence, rather than reacting automatically.

In the practice that is outlined below, we take the next step in undoing the habits of grasping and aversion by shifting attention gently *towards* the unpleasant experience. We practise this by 'being with it', neither getting sucked into the stories that drag us into rumination, nor trying to stop or avoid the feeling of what is troubling us. Instead, we move attention compassionately into the experience, effecting a transformation right in the moment. Remember to be gentle. If what comes up is overwhelming, this may not be the best practice for you right now. If in doubt, seek the guidance of an experienced mindfulness teacher.

1. Take an upright, dignified, relaxed sitting posture, and practise mindfulness of breathing for a few minutes. Follow this with a period of mindfulness of body practice, opening awareness to body sensations, as they arise.

2. Do you notice any unpleasant aspects of experience that are present at the moment? Are you feeling discomfort or pain

anywhere in the body? If so, where? What about difficult emotions? If there are some, ask yourself where they are and which sensations appear. Be aware of any tightness, pressure, restlessness, heat, throbbing and so on. Bring attention gently to the thoughts in your mind. Are these pleasant or unpleasant? Notice any reactions to arising sensations or thoughts. Are you tending to pull away from them, get annoyed by them, ruminate on them, or are you reacting in some other way? Without buying into them or trying to stop them, simply notice these reactions with kindness and interest.

3. Now, turn your attention towards an unpleasant sensation, a region of intensity in the body. It could be a subtle sensation or more pronounced. With gentleness, direct the mind's eye to this area and tune into what you find. Allow yourself to feel whatever sensation is there, softly. You could imagine breathing into the sensation as you inhale, and breathing out from it as you exhale, letting it be experienced with the rhythm and flow of the breath. Without trying to change it in any way, experiment with offering it a kind space in which to happen. See if you can let go of any attempt to eliminate it or distract from it. Just offer your curiosity, being with it, moment by moment. Is the sensation moving at all, shifting in location, intensity or quality? Notice any thoughts that arise in relation to the feeling, and let these pass through in the background of awareness, without trying to follow or stop them. Let go of trying to think your way out of the difficult experience. Just let it be, compassionately embracing it as warmly as you can.

CHAPTER SIX

To Study the Self ...

To study the way is to study the self.
To study the self is to forget the self.
To forget the self is to be enlightened by
all things of the universe.

Eihei Dogen[1]

In the summer of 2006, halfway through my year-long stay at Dechen Choling, I decamped to Canada for a month's retreat. Unlike the month-long programme I attended the year before, the emphasis this time was less on formal meditation practice and more on deepening an understanding of key Buddhist teachings. In some ways, this meant I was on more familiar academic ground, as participants were expected to study carefully beforehand, and the retreat itself included talks, debates and even a couple of exams.

But the similarities with my prior education ended there. The focus of investigation for this retreat wasn't any academic subject (not even Buddhism), but the very nature of being. And, although we were invited to use texts as pointers, the experiences to which they were pointing, and their practical implications for how to live wisely, could be confirmed only through a willingness to connect with direct experience. As the retreat leader informed us in his opening address, we would be invited to explore the question posed by Huineng back in the seventh century: 'What *is* it that thus comes?'[2] This was set not as an intellectual exercise, but to encourage engaged, embodied enquiry into what appears to the senses from moment to moment. In this way, Buddhist practice is far less religious than it is phenomenological – a heartfelt tuning to life that occurs by paying attention. Its purpose is to learn from what we find, so we can live more skilfully.

Buddhism proposes that a case of mistaken identity – the sense of being a definable, separate 'me' to whom life happens – is at the core of all stress and difficulty. Clinging to this fiction, which can be discerned through careful observation, is a root cause of suffering. When enquiring into the nature of things we must therefore examine not just experience but the experiencer – what we like to call 'me'. This 'me', it turns out, is not as definite as it seems.

Training attention is important for this enquiry, as it helps to focus consciously. But the capacity to pay attention is not in itself a guarantee of insight. 'Goats, sheep, cows, buffalos, camels and donkeys have attention,' said the wise man Nagasena, 'but they do not have wisdom.'[3] Opening to awareness, and relating to what happens in life from a place of kindly, connected observation, is more valuable in this endeavour. For when we discover that it's possible for thoughts, emotions and sensations to be observed in awareness, then we also realise that those thoughts, emotions and sensations cannot be the whole of who we are. Likewise, if we can be aware of habitual reactions to these aspects of inner process, then we are also learning that identity does not rest in those reactions either. So, is there *anything* in our ever-changing experience that we might legitimately call 'me' – in the sense of a single, central actor to whom everything happens? No one yet has been able to find one.

Stress reduction, preventing relapse into depression, developing resilience to cope with illness and adversity, greater cognitive and emotion regulation, improved relational skills, and an ability to make better, less bias-prone decisions, as well as many other life-enhancing benefits, all seem to flow from mindfulness training. But, from a Buddhist perspective, all of these can be seen as by-products of travelling along the path to a deeper enlightenment, which flows from the recognition of a key reality of existence – that *nothing* in the circumstances of our lives, including what we usually experience as ourselves, is stuck in the way we think.

Participants in an eight-week mindfulness course are introduced to the possibility that we can let go of our stories about stress and pain, learn that thoughts are not facts, and realise that sensations change from moment to moment. They may be invited to notice that experience is fluid, and can be perceived without taking it quite so personally. However, another question, which follows logically from all of this, is less likely to be addressed explicitly in standard mindfulness training. If pain, stress, thoughts and everything else that occurs in the mind and body are not 'me', then what kind of 'me' is there? Could it be that who I usually imagine myself to be – *my* thoughts and sensory experiences – never actually constitutes a solid, single, separate self? And if this is the case, what are the implications?

There are some good reasons why this enquiry isn't always pursued. An eight-week mindfulness course is usually too short to prepare for such a profound investigation. Habits of mind are built up and strengthened over the course of a lifetime (not to mention over the course of human evolution), so you would not expect them to be dissolvable in just two months. Mindfulness training requires space, stillness and sufficient slowing down to facilitate a new kind of learning, and only so much can be pointed to before what's being learned becomes just more concept, rather than embodied experi-ence – at which point it's likely to become less effective, or even a barrier to mindfulness.

Concerns are also expressed about the readiness of some people for this kind of investigation. When psyches are already fragile or brittle, can they confidently process the deep and radical shifts in perspective that are encouraged by this teaching, especially at an early stage of training? It could also be argued that teachers need not – or even should not – cultivate these shifts, given that the stated purpose of such courses is generally 'stress reduction', 'preventing relapse into depression', or some similar well-being related aim.

And yet, pursuing this deeper investigation can be highly rewarding, if not on an introductory eight-week course, then during follow-up learning streams for those who have developed a robust foundation in mindfulness. Also, the topic comes up anyway. Whenever a person sits down and brings attention to the breath, they start to observe the arising and dissolving of automatic thoughts in the space of the mind. As they come to recognise that 'thoughts are not facts' and 'you are not your thoughts', it's only a matter of time before a series of questions naturally arises. What are these thoughts and to whom do they belong? If 'I' am not bringing them about through the conscious decision to think them, where do they come from? And if they are not coming from me, and I am not my thoughts (or my emotions, or my sensations), then who on earth am I? We may not have signed up for an existential enquiry when we started training in mindfulness, but we get one anyway, because deep relief of symptoms comes through a reordering of our ways of seeing and of being.

When I navigated my life as 'someone who gets depressed', I limited the scope for a more flexible perspective that was not caught in self-identity. When a stressful life event occurred, in addition to unpleasant body sensations, it was easy to believe the thought that 'I' was falling into depression. Based on my previous experience of several severe and enduring episodes, this was the interpretation that was primed in my mind – depression happens to 'me'. This tended to provoke more automatic negative thoughts, such as: Oh no, here it comes again. It's awful and there's nothing I can do about it. It's all downhill from here. As I firmly believed that these thoughts were also 'mine', they offered even more evidence of 'my' oncoming episode, which by now seemed as threatening as the stressful event that had triggered them.

Panic and struggle would likely follow, experienced as even more uncomfortable sensations, and sparking even more negative thoughts. The depression would therefore become self-generating as 'my' thoughts and feelings became a thing called 'depression' from which 'I' suffered. It created a serious threat to my well-being, some*thing* to resist. So 'I' entered a vortex loop of feeling bad because I was believing negative, biased thoughts that came when I felt bad, which led to struggling with feeling bad, which led, of course, to feeling even worse – as I've tried to show, depression thrives on resistance. The more 'I' was caught in this loop, the more stressful it seemed, and the worse 'I' felt. And the worse 'I' felt, the more 'I' was depressed.

Some relief from this cycle can be gained by recognising that 'depression', and the thoughts and feelings that come with it, are not my identity – they don't define who I am. Allowing thoughts and sensations to be *as* they are, just arising and passing experiences in the mind and body, rather than things that define 'me', frees me from the unnecessary, extra suffering that is generated by fixating on them. When there is no 'I' to suffer from depression, there is no need to defend myself against it.

This sounds very strange to most people, because of course there is a you – just look and feel, *there* you are. There is no denying this, and the investigation into selfhood does not conclude with a discovery of nothing. We don't disappear in a puff of magician's smoke. Instead, when we look with insight, we learn that, like everyone and everything else that appear in the world, our so-called 'self' is in continuing transition from moment to moment.

If you ask people who they are, most of them will come up with a list of identities – perhaps a name, a profession, a family role, a nationality. I am Ed Halliwell, a mindfulness teacher, the father of two boys, British. It's a short list, but already there are problems. A name, as Jon Kabat-Zinn puts it beautifully, is 'just a sound that your parents gave to you when you were born'.[4] These may be applied consistently, for convenience, throughout a lifetime, but what they refer to certainly shifts over the years. Clearly, I am not the same 'me' who had my name as a baby. I am much larger, I have very different mental and physical capacities, a different perspective on the world around me, and a different relationship with the thoughts and feelings that arise in my mind. I am also not the same as the two-year-old 'me', or the five-year-old 'me', or even the thirty-five-year-old 'me' (when my list of identities might have included 'single with no children', 'city-dweller' and 'well-being researcher' – none of which still applies just a few years later). My opinions on politics, family life, religion and sport are now very different from those I held in earlier phases of life.

The composition of our bodies is in constant flux, too. Over the last few weeks, if I understand biologists correctly,[5] the epidermis (the layer of skin that covers your body) has completely regenerated. Cells in the stomach are replaced after about five days, while our livers regenerate every year. The cells in your rib muscles and gut have been entirely renewed over the last decade and a half, while your entire skeleton is replaced every ten years. Just as many of our beliefs develop over the decades, our bodies change, too. And if 'our' bodies change without 'our' permission, how much control do we really have over their workings? Our heartbeat, blood flow, bowel movements and every other automatic process all happen without conscious control, and – for as long as we remain alive – each of 'our' trillions of cells plays out its own life within us, just like each of the billions of neurons in 'our' brains.

The body's condition can have a great impact on our feelings, thoughts and actions. When tired, or sick, or in pain, do you meet the events of your life in the same way as when you are feeling energised and healthy? And while there are things we can do to nurture physical good health, to a large extent our bodies live their own lives, working well or poorly irrespective of our conscious decisions, and coming to an end of their lifespan at a time that is usually not of our choosing.

The brain changes all the time, too. Over the last fifteen years, researchers have learned that neural shifts occur in relation to events in the mind, body and life. So, for instance, an experienced London taxi driver will develop an unusually large hippocampus (a part of the brain associated with learning, memory and spatial processing),[6] while a skilled musician's fine motor cortex will reflect their years of practice and nimble fingers.[7] Even learning to juggle over the course of a week produces observable neural changes.[8] Just as everything that happens in the brain affects the experience of mind and body, so all of the mind's and body's experiences affect the brain, which is continually shaped by what we do and think, just as the body is shaped by our physical exercise. Many people believe that the core of their 'self' resides in the brain, but if we never have the same brain from one moment to the next, how could there be such a core?

In the 1960s, Roger Sperry carried out a series of experiments on people with severed forebrain commissures.[9] These are nerve tracts that connect the left and right hemispheres of the brain, and they have sometimes been surgically cut as a treatment for epilepsy. Sperry studied the behaviour of some of these patients, and found that while their actions seemed mostly normal, under certain conditions the left and right sides of their brains could act quite independently. Sperry was able to demonstrate this because different functions are controlled by the different brain hemispheres. So, objects from the left visual field are processed by the right side of the brain, which also controls the movement of the left hand, whereas language is usually controlled by the left hemisphere. Sperry found that if he partitioned off the visual field of his subjects, and showed an object only to the brain's right hemisphere, they would claim not to see anything. However, if he then invited them to touch the thing that they'd just claimed they could not see with their left hand, they would pick it up without hesitation. Yet these 'split-brain' patients still couldn't tell Sperry what they were holding, because the left hemisphere remained unsighted. Even more curiously, when their left hemisphere was shown the object (by placing it in the right side of their field of vision) and they were asked why their left hand had chosen to pick it up, they would often provide an apparently plausible (but clearly untrue) explanation that was entirely unrelated to what had just happened. Not only did the left side of the brain appear to have no knowledge of what the right was experiencing; it was prepared to fill in the gaps through invention.

Sperry was awarded a Nobel prize for his work, which suggests that the brain, when divided down the middle, is capable of working as two different entities, each with different memories, desires and ways of behaving. In other experiments with split-brain patients, two sides of the same brain have even been known to fight with each other, sending the left and right hands into battle.

Neuroscience has come a long way since Sperry's experiments, and its discoveries suggest that we are unlikely ever to find a 'self' within the brain. Everything that makes up our conscious experience seems to be associated with structure, activity and connections across the spectacularly complex workings of the brain, with its billions of neurons and trillions of synapses. Yet nowhere in the brain, just as nowhere in the body, is there a place we can point to and say: 'That's where *I* am'. As *Time* magazine concluded in 2002: 'After more than a century of looking for it, brain researchers have long since concluded that there is no conceivable place for a self to be located in the physical brain, and that it simply does not exist.'[10]

The evidence from neuroscience research suggests that what feels like 'me' is in fact an infinite number of changing aspects of mind, brain and body, working in harmony to produce a sense of coherence and agency from the events of life. The experience of being 'me' is a projection – a bit like when a film appears on a screen from the projection of different colours. The story of our life appears as if it is happening to 'me'. It may even seem that 'I' am directing it. But in reality, just as the split-brain patients' left hemispheres created plausible but false explanations for the actions of the right, so the projected 'me' assumes responsibility for actions that occur as a fluid interchange of indefinite aspects of mind, body, brain and environment.

Some experiments have suggested that the brain activity that corresponds to making a decision occurs *before* a person is consciously aware of choosing to do anything.[11] If your decisions are taken unconsciously, then are they really 'your' decisions? We like to think we are in charge of our lives, but from the workings of our bodies and brains, to our thoughts and feelings, and even to many of our actions, it seems that we are not.

The psychologist Dan Wegner has compared the workings of the so-called 'self' to the stage show of a master illusionist[12] whose greatest trick is to convince us that he or she exists. What we call 'me' is actually a flow of strongly conditioned tendencies, aspects of experience that arise together, based on what has come before and what is happening now. As the Buddhist scholar Gay Watson has said: 'I is a process.'[13] Or, in the words of Buckminster Fuller: 'I seem to be a verb.'[14]

It's not even as if the aspects of consciousness we call the 'self' are reliable. We have already seen how thoughts and emotions often reflect events inaccurately. Our memories are suspect, our perceptions are warped, and our interpretations are strongly influenced by the circumstances in which we find ourselves. Whoever and whatever we spend time with shape our life and the actions taken within it. Research by James Fowler and Nicholas Christakis shows that the choices we make are deeply affected by those around us.[15] For example, if one of our friends is happy, we are 15 per cent more likely to be happy ourselves. And if the friend of a friend is happy, even that increases our chance of happiness by 10 per cent. On the negative side, if one of our friends becomes overweight, we are three times as likely to become overweight ourselves. Opinions, values and even the experience of being ill can shift according to community norms.

How we perceive things depends on how we're primed. In one experiment, simply trying to unjumble a list of words that describe attitudes of impatience, aggression or rudeness influences people to act in those ways, while being primed with words that indicate patience and politeness leads people to act with those qualities.[16] And in Ellen Langer's famous study, the lives of nursing-home residents were transformed when they were taken to a retreat where the surroundings replicated those of the elderly people's youth, and where they were treated as fit and healthy.[17] Their memory, posture, vision and hearing all improved, according to objective measures, as did their subjective well-being.

The past primes us, too. We are conditioned by parental inheritance – gender, personality patterns and vulnerabilities to illness that formed during the meeting of our mother's egg and father's sperm and developed as we grew in the womb. Our lives are affected by what our mother ate and how she felt during pregnancy (which in turn are influenced by her own genetic, parental and environmental heritage) as well as by the unique circumstances of our birth and early years. The quality of our education, the effects of the natural, built and cultural environments where we have lived, and the major and minor misfortunes and traumas that befall us (and those around us) over the years all leave traces, inevitably influencing how we meet every new experience. As James Mark Baldwin said in 1902: 'The development of the child's personality could not go on at all without the constant modification of his sense of himself by suggestions from others. So he himself, at every stage, is really in part someone else, even in his own thought.'[18] We are also continually reliant for our survival and well-being on the surroundings that sustain us – we depend on everything from the air to the sun, food and shelter.

If so much about ourselves and our lives is dependent on our historical and environmental contexts, in what way can we meaningfully say that we operate as a self that is distinct from those contexts? Spinoza argued: '[People] are mistaken in thinking themselves free. Their opinion is made up of consciousness of their own actions and ignorance of the causes by which they are determined.'[19] Yet, despite all of the evidence that we are deeply interdependent, and rely heavily on not just what's within us but also what's around us, we still think and act as if there's a 'me' who controls 'my' life.

As with most of the mind's mental shortcuts, there are benefits to assuming the existence of definite, unchanging selves operating within a definite, unchanging world. For starters, it means much less work, at least in the short term. When a friend walks into the room, it's easier to assume that they are the same person now as they were last month, rather than consider what may have shifted in them since. Having made this assumption, we 'know' their preferences, likely behaviours and attitudes, and we can react to their presence without the need to engage in the difficult – and energy-consuming – job of seeing them anew in this and every future moment. The same goes for ourselves: we can become ever more comfortable in our opinions and habits, and avoid the uncomfortable experience of refraining from an established pattern of behaviour, or questioning an ingrained thought or attitude.

But there are heavy costs to this, too. You don't have to get depressed to witness how close identification with thoughts, emotions and sensations creates suffering. Every time we turn a thought into a fact in our minds, and then own it as 'mine', we ignore the reality that it was generated by myriad causes and conditions – most of which lie outside of our conscious control. When we identify with a thought, it becomes difficult to see its biases, and we become trapped in a virtual version of life, doomed to self-righteousness, paranoia, negativity or other patterns of distorted thinking, all of which may bear little or no relation to the world beyond our automatic appraisal of it.

Meanwhile, when we identify with emotion, we become prisoners of our moods, seeing the world through dark clouds (or rose-tinted glasses) without recognising that our feeling perceptions are also distorted. And when we get caught up with our bodies, we are completely at their mercy, destined to struggle with a journey through life that inevitably proceeds towards infirmity and breakdown. Acting in the vice-like grip of a self, we may fantasise our lives as autonomous, yet the very attachment to this fantasy creates bondage and resistance. We get stuck in a projected, fixated version of 'me', and then become annoyed when we are unable to control our lives.

Relief is attainable by shifting perception and letting go of the falsehood that we are in control. We can recognise that our experience is influenced by a vast range of causes and conditions, and that these shape our ability to respond. By tuning into and working with this reality – as it is felt through the senses, rather than as an idea in the head – we have more chance of recognising and relinquishing the habits that exacerbate stress, and of cultivating the choices that might helpfully affect our quality of life.

Wouldn't it make sense to drop the suffocating sense of personal accountability that many of us feel for everything that happens to us? Given that we live in a deep web of interconnection that is greatly determined by forces outside our control, might we not accept that much of our experience that arises in the moment – thoughts, emotions, sensations, reactive impulses – is not freely chosen, nor can it be easily and suddenly stopped or changed? By recognising the conditioning that deeply affects our lives, we can start to give ourselves – and others – a break.

At the same time, realising we are beings that change from moment to moment, in flow with an ever-shifting biological, psychological, social and environmental context, we can start to practise riding with the changes. Instead of expending energy on grasping for pleasure and resisting pain, we can feel those patterns in awareness but not be so consumed by them. We can hold our beliefs and opinions lightly, rather than construct blindingly fixed identities from them.

By developing greater alignment with the flow of change, we will have more energy to work with circumstances skilfully. We may have a limited range of choices due to the reality of our physical and mental condition, but there is still *some* free will. And, by tapping into awareness and relating to the world more from a place of sensing, we can expand that range of choices. Ironically, this comes from letting go of the need to run the show. The more we are able to recognise our limitations, the better we will operate among the current constraints of body, brain, mind and environment.

As soon as we are simply aware of thoughts and sensations

arising in experience, rather than caught up in attempts to grasp or reject them, a glimmer of space emerges between the events of our lives and our reactions to them. In this space, reactions can become responses. We enjoy some freedom to relate to what comes up and what to do next. By recognising that everything is constantly in flux, a state of basic ignorance transforms into clearer sight and the grasp of self diminishes. This can be a foundation and a guide for developing a different relationship with everything in life. When we recognise the ongoing change both within and around us, there is nothing solid to grasp or to fight against, and no one solid to defend. Tension and resistance fall away, along with the stress they generate. Life becomes a dance with the world, rather than a war against it; a flow, rather than a struggle. The Buddha described this state as true enlightenment, saying: 'Those who are not awakened grasp their thoughts and feelings, their body, their perception and consciousness and take them as solid, separate from the rest. Those who have awakened have the same thoughts and feelings, percep-tions, body and consciousness, but they are not grasped, not held, not taken as oneself.'[20]

When I first became depressed, I was outraged that such a state could descend on me, and that I seemed unable to do anything about it. As I viewed myself as the person in charge, it was easy to conclude that I must be to blame. This led to a desperate battle for change, which only generated more frustration. But when I rec-ognised my tendency to depression as a pattern in my physiology, psychology and life history that prompted automatic reactions to present-moment stress, I no longer felt so responsible for it. In other words, I didn't feel so bad for feeling bad – it was no longer personal. I could observe and experience what was happening with less sense of slight, and more dispassion, like a scientist looking into a microscope. At the same time, by recognising that depression is a passing rather than a permanent experience, I was freed from compounding the sense of helplessness and hopelessness that fuels the condition.

I now see 'depression' as just a name for a constellation of collid-ing, changing circumstances. Although it tends to recur, each new episode – and each moment – of depression is never the same as the last. I can observe this reality if I remember to tune in closely enough. By choosing not to buy into a fixed idea of what depression is (and always will be), I can experience it without a solid-seeming overlay that serves only to make it worse. It becomes possible to offer a gentle touch of compassion to what tends to feel heavy and constricting. That gentle touch is an antidote, lightening both the load itself and my habitual reactions to it. I am able to accept that the *story* of the depression – and of the 'me' who gets depressed – is an unhelpful, biased fiction. With ongoing practice of that shift in perception, increasing my recognition that I am neither completely in control nor completely helpless, I have developed more influence over how far I get trapped in depression, and what happens next.

This approach can be applied to every other aspect of life. Physical pain, difficulties in relationships, losing a job, unfair criticism, great worldly success and fortune, our most cherished opinions and beliefs, and even our inevitable ageing and death can all be held more lightly and seen more realistically if they are viewed as fluid rather than fixed. The Buddhist writer Stephen Batchelor offers a useful analogy for understanding this shift in perception: 'Gotama [Buddha] did for the self what Copernicus did for the earth: he put it in its rightful place, despite continuing to appear just as it did before ... [R]ather than regarding it as a fixed non-contingent point around which everything else turned, he recognised that each self was a fluid contingent process just like everything else.'[21]

Just as it appears to our eyes that the sun moves around the earth, we are strongly conditioned to see and feel ourselves as single, solid entities. Disengaging from this default mode is long and patient work. However, just as most people – after some education – are able to accept that the earth moves around the sun, it's possible to shift our self-image after some meditation practice. A study I mentioned earlier in Chapter Four, by Norman Farb and his colleagues at the University of Toronto, explored what happens in two distinct networks in the brain that seem to relate to our sense of self-reference.[22] One of these is the narrative – or default mode – network. Most people, most of the time, automatically use this network to process the stuff of the world. When it's active, our minds tell stories about ourselves and our lives, isolating themselves from direct, sensory experience by identifying with the internal commentary that turns experience into 'my' experience. When we are caught in the narrative network, we are stuck in planning, judging, categorising and reacting on the basis of our ideas of how things are. We are stuck in our thoughts, stuck in our heads.

By contrast, the second 'experiential' network is active when we are in touch with the felt sense of being, when we come down into our bodies. This network is activated when perception comes to us directly as sight, sound, feeling, taste and smell, unmediated by rumination, abstraction and preoccupation. When we let go of identifying with the merry-go-round of thoughts in our mind, we are less concerned with *surviving* life and more inclined to *live* it. We are more in tune with experience, both inside our bodies and in the world around us, without feeling the need to fight or grasp it. Conditioned thoughts, feelings and the events of life still occur, of course, but we are not so caught up in them. Indeed, when we are fully in tune, there is no 'me' to get caught up. There's just the flow of life. The meditation teacher Toni Packer has described the sense of being in this mode: 'I don't think in terms of having experiences anymore. Things just happen. Rain is dripping softly. The heart is beating. There is breathing in and out, in and out. There is quiet listening, openness ... emptiness ... nothing.'[23]

Most of us have known such moments. People often report experiencing such a state of union when they have relaxed in nature or felt deeply at peace in a lover's arms. But these experiences are difficult to invoke, because the very act of seeking them separates us from the acceptance on which they rely – as soon as we grasp for bliss it will not materialise, because the grasping will get in the way. We cannot search for contentment as a commodity. We have to let go into it.

Mindfulness facilitates this. As an old joke puts it: 'Enlightenment is an accident. But meditation makes you accident-prone.' According to Farb's studies, people who have taken mindfulness courses are more able to disengage from the narrative network and activate the experiential network. Invited to let go into sensing, they are able to draw on their meditation training, and their brain activity shifts accordingly.

There's a famous story in which the student Huike says to his teacher Bodhidharma: 'My mind is anxious. Please pacify it.'

Bodhidharma replies: 'Bring me your mind and I will pacify it.'

'I've tried to find it, but I cannot,' laments Huike.

'There – I have pacified your mind,' says Bodhidharma.

When we no longer get caught up in thoughts and sensations of anxiety, of frustration, of paranoia, of rejection, of rushing or of raging, we start to discover an equanimity that allows all of our mind- and body-states to play out as aspects of moment-by-moment experience, without needing to make them into a 'self' or fixating on them. By dropping our tight identification with what comes up in our minds, bodies and lives, we struggle less and we feel better. As Wei Wu Wei wrote: 'Why are you unhappy? Because 99.9 per cent of everything you think, and of everything you do, is for yourself – and there isn't one.'[24]

This approach is implied throughout any mindfulness-based stress reduction or mindfulness-based cognitive therapy course.

When students learn through practice that 'I am not my pain' or that 'thoughts are not facts', they start to shift from the narrative to the experiential mode. Instead of grasping for or resisting what happens, participants are invited to practise allowing things to be as they are in an ongoing flow of sensory experience, and to notice this with affection. This attitude of curiosity, laced with compassion, helps uncouple perceptions from the self-centred judgements and reactions that habitually accompany them, and which are the source of so much distress. Pain and difficulty still occur, of course, but those who are trained in a meditative approach do not get so caught in them.

Instead, we are invited to drop down further into experience itself. This turning towards what's happening, when approached gently and steadily, lightens our load as we discover a still place within – a place of non-reaction, non-striving, non-resisting. A sense of groundednesss occurs as ongoing experience is felt more centred in the body, and there is less of a tendency to default into our heads and our thoughts. This results in greater presence, and a less filtered view of life. We become more fully in touch.

So, far from being a fragmented, disconnected experience, letting go of the so-called self is a process of deep, ongoing, aware embodiment. It means relaxing into a flexible, integrated existence – one that does not demand constant fastening against the inevitable winds of change. The habit-driven struggle with life loses its intensity, leaving more openness, more presence, more light-heartedness, more joy.

The transformation of worldview invited by this experience is a lot to take in, so it's usually advisable to go slowly. It points to the root of the painful delusions to which we cling, and these are not easy to acknowledge, even when they are spelled out to us. After we have glimpsed them in our practice, we are still prone to clenching and closing off, again and again, especially when we feel threatened.

Yet practising and embodying this way of being – comprehending the realities of impermanence and selflessness – provide the fuel for a shift in perspective and approach that can lead to great relief. As Achaan Chah once put it: 'If you let go a little, you will get a little happiness. If you let go a lot, you will get a lot of happiness. And if you let go completely, you will be completely happy.'[25]

In Buddhist communities, there are programmes and practices that allow people to explore this in more depth, and it would be useful to develop more mainstream contexts to help the new wave of mindfulness practitioners investigate it further as well. Programmes like mindfulness-based stress reduction skilfully align well-established contemplative practices with an empirical, scientific worldview in a combination that speaks to the stresses of our age, in its own language. Practices like the body scan, mindful movement and sitting meditation invite interest into the nature of experience, encouraging participants to watch what happens when we let go of grasping and resistance, while simultaneously offering a training in groundedness that can always be returned to as a place of anchorage. Significant shifts in worldview can and do occur over the course of just eight weeks, relieving a lot of stress while excavating the topsoil of the self, perhaps in preparation for further work, once the student is ready. Because the shifts in the relationship with experience are invited deftly, they can occur at each participant's own pace.

Going deeper with the same approach is a practical next step after initial mindfulness training. All that's required is the willingness to observe and tune into the changing and interconnected nature of body, brain, mind and experience, and to experiment with living in recognition of this perspective. Below is a practice that will help to launch such an enquiry.

Practice to try: Resting in the flow

Bringing awareness to the flow of what we call the 'self' means recognising who we really are, and aligning our life with this truth. Being human is like flowing as a river – many moving droplets make up the stream, but only when they come together do they become the flow that is called a 'river'. The river changes constantly, yet there is continuity as it follows well-worn grooves through the landscape. A river cannot suddenly change its direction, and humans tend to follow a course set by past events and patterns. But the more we become aware of how the flow occurs and the grooves are followed, the more we can learn to work with the existing energy. We can start to influence our life's course. A good way to begin is by resting in the flow, and watching.

1. Settle into a posture for sitting meditation, feeling the connection of your body to the floor, cushion or seat. At any time during this practice, especially if you feel disconnected or disembodied, come back to this sense of groundedness, anchoring your experience to the earth.

2. Drop into mindfulness of breathing practice. Notice how each breath – indeed, each *moment* of each breath – is a unique experience, not the same as the previous one or the next. Yet there is also a sense of continuity, as the breath flows rhythmically in and out of your body. Notice how the breath happens without you controlling it – your breath is happening within you; 'you' are not choosing to breathe. Know, too, that all of the automatic processes of the body – oxygenation of the cells, blood flow, heartbeat

and so on – are happening along with the moment-by-moment flow of respiration, and that this is the very basis of being alive. All of it is happening without 'your' say-so. At the same time, by gently turning attention to the experience of breathing, moment by moment, you are exercising the capacity for directing the mind. It will likely wander off – another example of how life's events are conditioned without you – but once this is noticed, it becomes possible to return the mind to the breath. This demonstrates awareness – you know what's happening, as it's happening, at least some of the time. Try to relax into this experience, knowing that by working with the breath in this way, mindfulness is increasing. You are both recognising reality and working skilfully with this recognition.

3. Open awareness now to the whole body. As sensations rise into consciousness and pass through, recognise that they are all impermanent, continually transforming in intensity, location and quality. They are not an essence of 'you', any more than the breath is, although they also appear as aspects of conscious experience. Let them be experienced, moment by moment, and allow them to pass through without attachment or rejection. Recognise too that the physical constituents of your body are in flux – skin is being shed, cells are growing and dying, some neural connections are strengthening, others are weakening. The body is getting older and changing shape, whether 'you' like it or not.

4. Now bring awareness to thoughts. With a friendly interest, observe the patterns of thinking that are running through the mind. If it helps, you could see these thoughts as clouds passing across the sky of the mind, making up its weather.

The weather is always changing, depending on what is in the sky at any given moment. Consider that the thoughts you had a year ago, five years ago, a decade ago – each of which may have seemed extremely important back then – are now merely vague memories. The thoughts appearing in the mind right now will share that fate. Notice how the content of your thoughts – the language in which they occur, the vocabulary they use, the attitudes they adopt – is strongly conditioned by past events in your life, such as where you grew up and who raised you. Do your thoughts remind you of anyone else's voice? Ask yourself: Do you view your experiences differently now than you did five years ago, ten years ago, twenty years ago? If so, in what way? Reflect on the reality that every experience you have changes the composition of your brain, in which no 'self' resides. Imagine the vastly complex network of connections that produce the experience of 'your' mind – like a great neural orchestra in which no one instrument plays the lead.

5. Finally, open up your mindfulness to every aspect of conscious experience – sensations, sights, sounds, tastes and smells, thoughts and awareness itself. You don't need to make an effort to do this – just let go into the space within and around you, remaining alert and present to whatever comes. Allow the play of experience to happen by itself, resting in the flow, moment by moment. When you notice attention wandering to a particular place, acknowledge the wandering and open out to the whole panorama of experience once more. Continue to recognise the flow of experience for as long as you can.

What happens to depression
when I let go of me …

Feeling overwhelmed is a common trigger for my anxiety attacks. A project doesn't go as well as I'd hoped or I miss a deadline, and fear and insecurity rise in my mind and body. 'I'm going to be judged and found wanting,' goes the narrative. 'They won't want to work with me again. Who was I anyway to take on such a job? I'm an imposter. I always fall at the last hurdle.' My heart starts racing, my stomach churns, my muscles stiffen. These sensations are unpleasant, so I tense up further in an unconscious attempt not to feel them, even while my attention is pulled in their direction. Oh no, says a new thought. Why am I getting so anxious and blocked.

With so much energy expended internally, there's less available to attend to daily matters. Panic may set in. 'Now I can't get any other work done,' my mind laments. 'It's the old cycle downwards again. I'm cursed with depression.' The familiar pressure builds up in my nose and chest, making it difficult to access any other feelings, and the negativity starts to spiral: I won't be able to cope, I'll be left with no money, no energy, unable to dig myself out of this hole. The doom-mongering thoughts fuel even more anxiety. It could go on indefinitely – a self-fulfilling prophecy.

But hang on a minute. If these thoughts are just thoughts – and probably mere projections, tainted by the negative bias that comes especially at times of stress – then there's no need to follow them. Anxiety is a feeling, and I know that feelings come and go. Yesterday's thoughts and feelings were different, so who's to say my internal weather isn't due another change? There are patterns of experience, for sure, but this moment is just a constellation of events coming together in the mind, body and outside world. Ideas in the mind are in flux, sensations in the body are in flux, and the trigger events are already receding into memory – no more than traces of causal energy that set the winds of mental and physical habit blowing. Suddenly, with this shift in perspective, thoughts and feelings are no longer facts, and there's not even a solid, single, separate 'me' to feel upset or hurt by them. There is just experience, happening on and on. It's painful experience right now, to be sure, but just moments in motion nevertheless. I'm changing from moment to moment, too – everything is in flow, as it always is. This won't stay the same, and nor will I.

Rainer Maria Rilke once said: 'Let everything happen to you: beauty and terror. Just keep going. No feeling is final.'[26] We can make it even less personal. Just let everything happen (drop the 'to you') – watch and feel each aspect of the mind–body–world show play out on the stage of consciousness, experiencing it all with interest and kindness in the knowledge that the moment is already and inevitably on its way to becoming something else. If this moment is allowed to play out by itself, the next moments are less likely to be conditioned by misguided attempts to turn what is flowing into something solid, or to push away what is here, creating resistance to it. Neither solidifying nor separating from the moment can ever be successful, because the moment is always both here and in transition. But if there is no depression to get stuck in, and no self to get hurt, then everything in mind, body and life can flow like an undammed river, streaming through unfettered by the defensive psychic barriers that serve only to block the flow.

Negative thoughts – as well as the bodily symptoms of fear – may still be present. But they are not 'mine' any more. They just *are* – present remnants of past events that do not need to be turned into unnecessary future suffering. By shifting perspective and approach – experiencing without grasping and resistance – this moment has already become different from how it might have been.

CHAPTER SEVEN

Taking the Red Pill

After this, there is no turning back.
You take the blue pill – the story ends, you
wake up in your bed and believe whatever
you want to believe. You take the red pill –
you stay in Wonderland and I show you
how deep the rabbit-hole goes.

Morpheus to Neo, *The Matrix*[1]

My favourite place to meditate these days is in the churchyard next to our house. The church is a thousand years old, and there's a sense of sacred space about the building and the surrounding land, perhaps connected to its long tenure as a place of reflection and worship. The gravestones range from the very recent to the very old, with some so ancient that you can no longer read the names and dates. To the south there are the rolling Sussex Downs, hills undulating into the sky. It's a rare place of quiet in hectic times.

Sitting propped by a tree trunk, drinking in the landscape, I find mind and body merge easily with each other, and with the environment. In the stillness, there's awareness. There's also attunement, not just to what's going on in the realm of the interior, but to how this is inextricably woven into the surrounding world. Sitting here in silence evokes connection, coherence, congruence.

In the development of mindfulness-based cognitive therapy, John Teasdale, Mark Williams and Zindel Segal identified two modes through which humans tend to operate. The 'doing' mode relies on conceptual processing. Having evolved the capacity to think, human beings are able to relate to the world through abstract ideas. This brings great power, because it frees us from dependence on moment-to-moment experience as the only propeller to action. Unlike most animals, we can plan ahead, think back, motivate ourselves to achieve goals, and formulate reasoned explanations and decisions. The capacity to think in this abstract way is the source of many of humanity's great achievements – it has led us to heart bypass surgery, space exploration, the internet, all of the world's literature, and structuring societies based on principles of justice and democracy.

Because the doing mode abstracts us from sensory experience, it enables us to make meaning from what happens. When things are not how we would like them to be, we can ponder the situation. We might wish for things to be different, perhaps formulate strategies for how they might be changed, or interpret events with a view to identifying their causes, so we might avoid them in the future. We can hope that pleasant events might occur more often too, and fantasise about how we might make that happen. We can even analyse our analyses with the aim of becoming more effective in our quest for pleasure. Rather than simply feeling and reacting in our bodies to pleasure and pain, the doing mind ruminates on what is happening. This can give rise to anxiety and discontent that go far beyond the sensation of pain, or the physicality of an instinctive reaction.

While abstract reasoning is useful for the resolution of some difficulties – such as a broken-down car – other problems are not so easily rectified in this way. Chronic illness, ageing, unwelcome emotions and automatic reactions are not eliminated by thinking about them. Indeed, trying to deal with these kinds of issues by devising and following strategies to avoid or resolve them may highlight the gulf between what we want to happen and what *is* happening. It's easy to get caught in a cycle of pushing for satisfaction, relentlessly striving for happiness that can't be found by trying to eliminate, change or prevent the inevitable difficulties that come with being alive. Instead, the unfulfilled striving for happiness itself ramps up dissatisfaction, leading to more tension, more craving and aversion, more suffering, more thinking and strategising, and so on.

This happened to me whenever I became anxious. In a frantic quest to be rid of unpleasant experiences, my mind revved up its search for answers. But soon I felt depressed and more anxious, because the thinking or action failed to produce the desired solution. My mind would spiral into judging, blaming, criticising and reasoning. I was stuck in a loop – driven to distraction, caught in abstraction, desperate to flee from my own life. My mind seemed to be at war with my body – and at war with the world.

Though we are blessed with an intelligence that is not shared by other animals, the complex capacity for abstract thought draws humans away from the simple, sensory experience of the present moment. Rather than a coherent, connected, congruent consciousness, characterised by a rolling flow of experience and reaction, we tend to dwell in a self-made prison of thoughts, connected to the events of the world only through walls of concept. Like Mr Duffy in James Joyce's *Dubliners*, we live a few feet from our bodies. We are, as Achaan Chah characterised the Western world, 'lost in thought'.[2]

This condition of distraction is stressful and maladaptive. Fragmentation is not conducive to flourishing. When mind and body are at war with each other, the body reacts as if it is under attack from a predator, so we don't feel good. Meanwhile, the mind becomes that crazed predator, out of touch with reality, aggressive, frazzled. As anyone who has experienced depression or anxiety knows, it becomes much more difficult to attend to the fundamentals of life in this state, because the body that perceives danger is so freaked out, and because there's so much shouting in the head that you can barely concentrate on anything else.

Of course, it's impossible to turn back evolution. But, as the Buddha's third and fourth noble truths suggest, there is a way of transforming our experience by cultivating a different relationship with it. Along with feeling and thinking, humans can be aware, resting in a space that recognises and works more skilfully with both thought and sensory experience. By opening ourselves to thoughts and feelings in awareness, there no longer needs to be a fight between them. They may still be experienced as unpleasant, but when neither is identified as the 'truth' of what is happening, we don't get so caught up in reacting automatically. When everything that's happening is allowed to be present without any attempt to avoid it, there will be no struggle. Every event can coexist in the space of the wide, wise awareness that experiences it. Thus, the war of reaction subsides.

Meditation practice helps us drop down from the fragmented complexities of the doing mind into the sensory experience of life on the ground. Teasdale, Williams and Segal call this the 'being' mode, and mindfulness training develops it. In the being mode, we can consciously direct our attention to a specific aspect of experience, and return to it when we notice the mind has wandered. Mostly we practise focusing on the body's senses, because our habit is to remain within the head. Buddhist psychology speaks of six senses – the familiar five, plus thought. Yet, do we give equal attention to all six? Hardly! We continually wander into thought.

Awareness helps us to notice that wandering and restore balance. As we become more familiar with patterns, and gently work to let them go, the relationship between thinking and sensing becomes less dysfunctional. We become more synchronised beings, more in tune internally, and more in tune with the world around us. Rather than being identified with just some of what's happening (usually our thoughts), and turning that into 'me', we come to rest with the whole of how things are right now. Awareness brings acceptance and peace.

As I gradually discovered through my practice, this can happen even when our experience is difficult, our animal urges are on fire, and our thoughts have gone spiralling into past and/or future. Awareness lets all of this happen and we see it, connecting with it in the here and now. The space that awareness offers doesn't judge, blame, criticise or reject. Therefore, awareness is unconditionally kind and compassionate – it gently embraces whatever occurs in its space. Dropping into awareness, a reintegration occurs that heals the psychic split.

This is how meditation has helped my recovery from depression. In showing me a way to give up the struggle for instant solutions to unpleasant states, the practice has enabled me to drop the battle between how I'd like to feel and how things actually are. Solution-focused thoughts still come, but I'm not so attached to them. So they don't provoke such resistance in my body, which is thus allowed to feel whatever it feels. Instead of prolonged anxiety and depression, I experience the appropriate feeling states for whichever difficulty is happening in my life at that moment. I might feel angry or sad for a while, but I no longer find myself caught in a low-mood loop.

Sometimes non-practitioners suggest that meditation is passive. But by repairing the rending of mind and body, and reducing our tendency to categorise people and things into fixed ideas of who and what we are for and against, meditation is one of the most radically transformative endeavours we can undertake. If we continue to be driven to solve the problem of suffering, even for the greater good, and if we remain stuck in a mode of mind that isolates us from parts of ourselves, others and the rest of the world, our actions probably won't be much help, because these divisions are the roots of suffering in the first place. It is in the practice of coming to stillness, acceptance, appreciation and presence that we find integration, and thus transformation. As Blaise Pascal wryly noted: 'All of humanity's problems stem from man's inability to sit quietly in a room alone.'[3] In the space of stillness, healing starts to happen by itself. Just as muddy water becomes clearer when it isn't stirred, so human clarity comes when we stop rushing around. But most of us do not know, or do not remember, how to sit quietly. We are bombarded by calls to action, whether from family, work, advertising, politics, our inner monologue or our bodily impulses. This is why meditation is helpful – it cultivates the conditions that lead to peace. We need to let things settle.

And when we have settled, awareness shows us what is here. It's just like looking into a mirror. If we are tense, in pain, driven, distracted, frustrated, suppressed or depressed, it will reveal that non-judgementally. I have often dropped into meditation from a period of overactivity or overthinking to discover a sense of being blocked, agitated, contracted and pressured. However, as I stay with this sensation, it gradually gives way to energetic release, initially in the form of yawning, then with heaving breath, rushes of eupho-ria and manic, creative activity. In the midst of this unblocking, I'll often feel heart palpitations, irritability, stomach churning, impulses to run, eat, and write down my thoughts, as well as dis-traction and lethargy. Whatever I'm experiencing in the moment feels unending. Eventually, though – if I stay with it – a steadier sense of equanimity and peace arrives.

Without the method of meditation, it would be easy to get lost in all of this. But by gently harnessing attention, we can choose where to place our minds in the moment, returning to a soft focus again and again. Awareness shows us what's present, with a kindness we rarely show ourselves. Practising staying present to experience, moving gently towards what we find rather than clinging to or running from it, we are more able to stay connected to the here and now. (By contrast, the doing mode would have us scattering into thought, and into evasive or grasping action.) Tuned into our bodies, we are connected via the senses to phenomenal reality. Aware of thoughts, but not controlled by them, we are freed from distraction. Dropping into awareness, letting everything flow through it, we are in tune with the truth of our changing being, no longer trying to push the river of consciousness, or freeze it into a solid 'self'. We can rest in the current.

Mihaly Csikszentmihalyi, the psychologist who popularised the term 'flow', says: 'Happiness is the state of mind in which one does not desire to be in any other state.'[4] As soon as we try to get happy, we have moved out of the state of open appreciation that enables it to occur. Even worse, the drive to fulfil desire exhausts us, and we become more prone to stress and its consequences. In other words, to be happy, we must give up the search for happiness, because the search makes us miserable. The way to be happy as conscious beings is to rest in awareness. Or, as St Francis of Assisi put it succinctly, 'The one you are looking for is the one who is looking.'[5]

To be genuinely happy, we cannot shield ourselves from any part of life, including our inevitable difficulties and death. It's said that the Buddha's own path began when he came face to face with the reality of sickness, ageing and dying for the first time. Any way of mindfulness that fails to connect us to these realities cannot be called complete. 'It really puts perspective on things, though, doesn't it?' says Nigel Tufnell in *This Is Spinal Tap*, when standing beside Elvis Presley's grave at Graceland. 'Too much, there's too much fucking perspective now,' replies his bandmate David St Hubbins.[6] This is the usual human response to difficult truths: don't dwell on them, move on, keep going.

It's an approach that can work for a while, but ultimately its effects are unhelpful. Closing ourselves off from the mysteries of the universe, we may not have to contemplate unsettling realities such as death, but we also remove ourselves from the awesome. Our necks remain cricked downwards as we preoccupy ourselves with whatever immediate concerns lay ahead. We scuttle about like worker ants, thinking and doing our way through each day, oblivious to our place in the universe. Our gaze is lowered to the basic concerns of everyday living – what's for dinner, what's happening at work, why does my leg hurt, why won't my neighbour stop making that weird noise at night?

A *New Yorker* cartoon shows a surprised diner opening a fortune cookie that reads: 'Someday you will die.'[7] If ageing, sickness and death are inevitable, shouldn't we prepare for all three? This is challenging, of course, because it means tolerating hard realities and great uncertainties that can seem to threaten who we like to think we are. But, as Franz Kafka wrote, 'You can hold yourself back from the sufferings of the world, that is something you are free to do and it accords with your nature, but perhaps this very holding back is the one suffering you could avoid.'[8]

Mindfulness training, when we open fully to it, is an antidote to this holding back, because nothing is excluded from our awareness – we are willing to show an interest in everything. Jon Kabat-Zinn says: 'Meditation is not for the faint-hearted, or for those who routinely ignore the whispered longings of their own hearts.'[9] The price is our willingness to recognise, process and accept the realities (and uncertainties) of our lives. But the rewards are great because when we let ourselves be touched by these realities and uncertainties, we may find the power to rest in them contentedly, without creating suffering through denial and resistance.

During one of my month-long retreats at Dechen Choling, I gasped in the outdoor shower one morning as I was struck by the weirdness of being there at all. There I was, washing my body with water on the grass, with no real idea of how I, the water or the grass got there. Or, indeed, where it was all going next. In Martin Heidegger's vivid term, I was aware of feeling 'thrown' – utterly ignorant of the wider context for my life (if there was one) and with no apparent prospect of a certain explanation. The gasp was followed by a laugh – at the ridiculousness of being in such a scenario – and a sense of acceptance. Okay, so be it. Let's just keep exploring, with the amazing and mysterious capacity for awareness that enables us to make the journey a conscious one.

One of the consequences of mindfulness entering the mainstream has been the growth of its use in a range of mundane settings – from healthcare to education to business. Indeed, because mindfulness training is a way of working with the mind and body that can be rewarding in most situations and most environments, it makes sense that the advantages can be felt and seen in these domains. We bring the quality of our attention to everything we do, so every aspect of our daily life can benefit when we pay attention in a more embodied way. However, we might miss out on a bigger prize if we view mindfulness merely as a means of getting through day-to-day life. If we can connect to the vast space of the world, we can hold our daily troubles more spaciously. You will know this space if you've ever looked up at the stars during a difficult time and felt the relief that comes not from any easing of your problems, but from a sense of their place within the vast magnificence and mystery of the universe. As The Dhammapada puts it bluntly: 'Many do not realise that we here must die. For those who realise this, quarrels end.'[10] Studies suggest that awareness of mortality leads to a sense of appreciation – people who are invited to imagine their own death report an increase in gratitude.[11] We are 40 per cent more likely to help a stranger in a graveyard than on the street.[12]

Before I knew how to meditate, I suffered from a kind of existential nagging in my chest, but it was thick with depression. I would watch games of football on television but I was unable to enjoy them because they seemed pointless. After all, didn't they just start from scratch again each season? So why should I care who won? Disconnected from any sense of heartfelt values, following my most basic urges from moment to moment, I didn't have the capacity to face and hold difficult realities, and the feelings that accompanied them. Automatically stuffing them down was a way to avoid connecting with these greater questions, but that incurred the cost of feeling heavy, directionless and unfulfilled. It was perhaps no coincidence that my favourite comedy at the time was *Seinfeld* – a show in which 'nothing happens' and the four main characters are caught in a state of suppressed existential crisis that never quite rises to the surface. The following conversation from the show stuck in my mind:

KRAMER: Do you ever yearn?

GEORGE: *Yearn?* Do I yearn?

KRAMER: *I* yearn.

GEORGE: You yearn?

KRAMER: Oh, yes. Yes, I yearn. Often I sit ... and yearn. Have you yearned?

GEORGE: Well, not recently. I crave.[13]

This is a recipe for a life of desperation. But it doesn't have to be that way. As I began to enter my practice, softening my hard heart and connecting my flesh to the world around, sitting and opening myself to the senses, I started to hear the yearning beneath the craving, and nihilism was replaced by meaningful enquiry. I started to find this experience of the world interesting, rather than running from it or trying to capture it. From this perspective, the tears in my early days of practice were like melting ice in my body, which had frozen to protect me from all of the difficult truths of living. But that had inevitably left me rigid and cold.

Opening up to the whole of life, we build the resilience to live it well. People who lead more meaningful lives tend to be happier in the long run,[14] even though, like most people, they will experience times of difficulty. Although I was deeply unhappy when stuck in depression, I never seriously contemplated taking my own life, mainly, I believe, because I never lost a sense of my life – including my experience of depression itself – as basically meaningful. Although it was sometimes difficult to hear them beneath the chaotic chattering of thoughts and the anguish in my body, the 'whispered longings' of my heart were never stilled, and eventually I started to listen to them. The world seemed to be calling me to life, day after day, even though being alive was deeply unpleasant at the time. In a way that I didn't quite understand, I remained connected to this world and I wasn't prepared to leave it.

Tuning in like this requires no religious faith – indeed, belief without evidence gets in the way, fixing us in opinions rather than leaving us open to the basic phenomena that appear. To access it as fully as possible, we must let go of dogma and instead remain open to the senses, willing to notice whatever comes. We can give up the consolation of stories based on faith without evidence, and accept the reward of opening to the world as it actually appears.

What do we find when we allow this to happen? First, we notice that everything is changing. Just as there is no solid self to cling to, so everything in the world is in transition. From the smallest microbes to the greatest stars in the universe, nothing is permanent. Nothing is immune to the process of change – our planet, like everything else, is different from moment to moment, and it will pass away some day. This applies to ideas as much as it does to material bodies – no thought, no culture, no movement has ever lasted for ever, or indeed for more than the moment it takes to change into something new. The world is always fresh because everything is constantly emerging and dissolving.

There is the reality of connection. Thích Nhất Hạnh has coined a word to describe this state: 'interbeing'.[15] A rose cannot exist without the sun, earth and rain that nurtures it into being, and it cannot be experienced without someone to sense it. This is true of everything in the appearing universe – none of it occurs without causes and conditions to make it happen. The air you breathe, the food you eat, the clothes you wear, the home where you live, the language you speak, the thoughts you have and the actions you undertake all depend on a vast array of inter-arising influences that have brought them into being, and without which they could not possibly be what they are. Your body is part of a mysterious evolutionary march from the Big Bang to your birth and beyond – from the first appearance of stardust to the cells of your body today, with all of history lying in between. Consider, as you breathe in, that the oxygen molecules in the air that sustains you were probably once exhaled by Julius Caesar.[16] As Bill Bryson put it: 'Every atom you possess has almost certainly passed through several stars and been part of millions of organisms on its way to becoming you.'[17]

Nothing in this world can exist in isolation, because each aspect has emerged from the connecting of causes and conditions. And because every thing is impermanent, it is already interacting, changing and reforming in relationship with the world around it, which in turn is changing in relationship with *its* surrounding world. There is a vast web of causes and conditions that connects everything to everything else. Plants breathe out, we breathe in. We breathe out, plants breathe in. One couldn't happen without the other. Everything is entwined. We are all in it together.

When I'm sitting in the churchyard, awake, there is no single, separate, solid 'me', and I am perceiving no 'objects', as all of these are made up of processes that occur moment by moment in relation to one another. We give these processes names that appear to separate them, such as air, clouds, automatic thoughts and emotions – yet all of it happens in harmony, like a brilliant orchestra without a conductor. This is both a great joy and a great relief, because nothing needs to be done to make it more than it already is. And as long as the doing mode 'me' allows it to happen without interference, it's stress free. As the poet Rumi wrote:

> Out beyond ideas of wrongdoing and rightdoing,
> there is a field. I'll meet you there.
> When the soul lies down in that grass,
> the world is too full to talk about.
> Ideas, language, even the phrase *each other*
> doesn't make any sense.[18]

In this field, the experience of well-being goes well beyond stress reduction. It is bliss. But, as Rumi suggests, it is indescribable – trying to turn it into language, attempting to solidify it into an idea, reduces it to concept.

It's all rather wonderful if we are willing to appreciate it. But, of course, we are not willing, most of the time. William Blake famously wrote: 'If the doors of perception were cleansed, everything would appear to man as it is, infinite. For man has closed himself up, till he sees all things thro' narrow chinks of his cavern.'[19] Things are in-finite (not limited, not separate), but we fail to appreciate this, because we identify mainly with the thinking mind, abstracting everything into concepts, rather than connecting through the senses, which are the font of direct perception. We get caught in our lives, rather than experiencing them with awareness.

During the early weeks of a mindfulness course, participants are invited to spend a week noticing one pleasant moment each day and recording the thoughts, emotions and sensations that arise in relation to that event. The practice reveals how simple joys are easily available to – yet easily missed by – most of us. Our habitual bias for noticing and remembering the negative, which is helpful in alerting us to life-threatening situations, orients us away from savouring the pleasant. Yet, missing the readily available beauty around us actually damages our well-being. Emotions such as awe and joy have been linked with a lower level of pro-inflammatory cytokines, which is considered a marker of good health, [20] as well as reduced anxiety and depression, and greater satisfaction with life. [21]

The pleasant events that we notice are usually appreciations of nature (sunsets, gardens, walks in the woods) or relationships (a smile from a child, a kind word from a colleague, meeting an old friend). Rarely do they incur a direct monetary cost, or require great effort to find. Instead, they must be received in awareness, unfettered by hurry or worry. The easy availability of these pleasant events for most of us in the Western world gives the lie to the culturally sanctioned belief that happiness comes with conventional markers of success or an abundance of possessions. As Allen Ginsberg once said: 'You own twice as much of the rug if you're twice as aware of the rug.'[22] Abundance can be found even in hardship, with the ability to attend with interest.

Among adults, the pleasantness of simple events often evokes surprise. This is probably because the wide availability of wonder is forgotten somewhere in the midst of youth as we start to devote more time and thought to our increasing responsibilities. The demands of maturity squeeze out the curiosity of childhood, as if showing an interest in the world – which requires slowing down enough to look at it – were a childish impediment. In a culture that values striving for possessions and luxuries beyond basic need, children are often 'hurried up' when they linger on some delight of nature. No wonder they soon start to strive themselves, as the capacity for complex reasoning – the doing mode – grows within them.

Choosing to appreciate natural wonder opens us up to the magic of ordinary experience. This isn't just positive thinking – a desire for things to be pleasant when they're not. It's a willingness to connect with the wonder of the world that presents itself to our senses, as we feel it in our bodies.

Equal time on a mindfulness course is given to noticing unpleasant events. These tend to be found more readily, as our habitual bias for spotting threats brings them quickly and starkly into focus. Our bodies' survival mechanisms produce alerts in the form of painful sensations, and the thinking mind produces automatic thoughts that demand quick resolution. Nevertheless, when these events are experienced openly, there's an unhooking from the additional stress of trying to shut them out or becoming overwhelmed by them. We discover that facing the inevitable pains of life frees us from the avoidable ones. Open to the pleasant and the unpleasant, we are in a position to live more fully, more completely, more awake.

Meditation is a tool that helps us wake up. This is what is meant by the term 'Buddha' – one who is awake. According to the Buddhist diagnosis, the normal human condition is to go through life in a state of sleep, reacting automatically (and therefore unconsciously) to the problems of living because it's easier to do this than face reality. This approach confers a degree of protection from the anxiety of acknowledging our mortal situation, but it means living from little awareness. Our view is dim, and we tend to get stuck in venal habits and petty projects. We have a slim chance of working with life consciously.

However, if we can really live the mystery, lean into it fully with the senses, then we can start to reclaim our faculty of wonder. We can be amazed by the fact that we are alive – as billions of atoms that can somehow be aware of themselves. What we lose in false certainty, we gain a hundredfold in humility, curiosity and flexibility. Whatever the reality or otherwise of rebirth from one life to the next, we experience the reality of rebirth from one moment to the next.

A Zen student once asked his master what happens after death.

The master shrugged his shoulders and said: 'I don't know.'

'But you're a Zen master,' protested the student.

'Yes,' he said, 'but not a dead one.'

Another Zen master, Thích Nhất Hạnh, points out that you don't need to fly in the air or walk on water to witness a miracle – walking on the earth is remarkable enough.[23]

Although my intuition tells me that death is not the end, and I have experienced flashes of what seem to be past-life memories, I don't know what these thoughts and feelings really are, or from where they originate. Meditation practice has shown me many times that thoughts and feelings arising in my mind and body do not align with phenomenal events, especially as seen by others, so I know my interpretations cannot always be trusted. We expect the sun to rise tomorrow, but this is based only on evidence from previous mornings. We have no guarantees that it will continue to happen. We don't even know how thoughts are created – they just pop up in awareness, often unbidden. Philosophers and scientists call consciousness the 'hard problem', which basically means that none of them has a clue where it comes from and why it's present. It's more difficult to allow mystery to remain mysterious, rather than try to find explanations for everything, but to me it feels more healthy and honest.

In meditation practice, we relinquish the fantasy that we have full control, and in return we receive the reward of not having to have it altogether, of not having to be constantly judging and blaming ourselves and everyone else for every unwelcome thought, feeling and action. Instead of struggling with an opinionated version of ourselves, others and the world, we can recognise the flow of experience of which we are a part, feel that part fully, and drop our resistance to what we cannot control, which is most of it. In 'The Marriage of Heaven and Hell', William Blake describes what will happen when we experience things fully: 'The whole creation will be consumed and appear infinite and holy where it now appears finite and corrupt. This will come to pass by an improvement in sensual enjoyment.'[24] Wholeness (holiness) and infinity (non-limitation) are found, says Blake, by experiencing everything with the senses.

When the symptoms of stress strike, opening myself up to the world provides an antidote, whereas closing down merely tightens the grip of tension. I know that the unpleasant thoughts and sensations that dominate my experience in that moment are impermanent, along with everything else. The inner troubles I cared deeply about five years ago are today just memories, and it's likely that today's stress will be the same five years down the line. I also know that stressful thoughts and sensations occurring within me are created by patterns of reaction bequeathed by evolution, and influenced by both my personal history and the history of the world itself. This makes me feel less responsible for them, and less prone to try to eradicate them – two responses that only ever make them stronger.

We often fail to see the beauty in life because we have evolved to be on the lookout for threats, which are then magnified in our minds and resisted. Moreover, everyone around us also focuses on threats, which establishes a social and cultural reinforcement loop that further impels us to do the same. We are so busy trying to control the world, or trying to run away from it, that it rarely occurs to us to stop and appreciate it.

So it helps to make space for being present. This is the mode we invite in meditation – a dropping out of the gears of doing and thinking, and into a lingering with the events of the moment themselves. With this lingering, this being, we are able to *receive* these events, rather than just react to them. Nothing is left out, as we bear witness to everything that arises in the open space of awareness. For a while at least, we can experience everything as it passes through in peace.

Making space for being

For millions of years, animals have lived in tune with the world. Living through the senses, untroubled (as far as we know) by complex thinking, they just 'are' – present to the events of their lives, reacting to them intuitively. Sometimes people say to me: 'My cat's really mindful. It just sits there, present, experiencing the moment.' But the cat isn't mindful. It's just being a cat, automatically resonating with the world around it, perhaps, but probably unconsciously so. Mindfulness doesn't turn us back into animals; it doesn't flick a switch and turn off the thinking mind. It embraces thinking as an aspect of our whole experience. Being mindful invokes an aware, awake connection with the world that enables us to be knowingly present. We can use the human capacity for thinking to set an intention, redirecting our focus again and again, and opening ourselves to awareness as a way of holding all of whatever is happening. Rather than trying to split experience into separate parts, solidifying it into fixed entities, we can notice and flow with it all, consciously present to things as they are. This is 'being'.

But most of us aren't very good at 'being' like this. When we try to be still, most of us get restless, irritated or bored, or we start thinking, planning, wondering or wandering. Sometimes we even try to work out why we can't just 'be'. This is because we have inherited the doing mode of mind as our default. Paradoxically, then, getting into being mode requires some preparation. It starts by reconnecting with the body, the home of the senses. As partially conscious beings, we can do this deliberately, perhaps through mindfulness of breathing or the body scan. We train in directing and redirecting attention, and opening ourselves to the awareness that notices mind wandering. We can choose to unhook for a while from thinking.

The training continues as we practise staying present to whatever appears – both pleasant and unpleasant – meeting what happens with a friendly approach. We learn to let be, resting in wholeness even when fragmenting thoughts arise. Accepting these thoughts rather than identifying *as* these thoughts, we allow them in awareness. Experiencing everything in awareness, we notice the patterns within us and around us, recognising – and more intuitively in touch with – the realities of impermanence and interdependence. The more we train in these practices, the more we are able to rest in stillness without resistance, even when brought face to face with the difficult truths of life – sickness, ageing, pain and death. This brings relief from suffering. Thoughts and feelings – both unpleasant and pleasant – can be allowed to move through us, without so much of the grasping and resistance that heighten stress.

Now we may be ready for what is called 'choiceless awareness' – a compassionate abiding with everything that manifests in mind, body and life. As an expression of being, the practice of choiceless awareness invites a letting go from striving to possess, achieve or acquire what we want, and from resisting, denying or running away from what we don't like. We practise just *being* with whatever we find, experiencing in awareness the moment-by-moment flow of life without separating everything and everyone into this and that, them and us, must-have and must-get-rid-of.

This approach to life is very different from the one we find in our thinking minds and in our wider culture. Hence, practising it is sometimes viewed as a waste of time, passive or even selfish. We are ruled by the doing mode, which cannot conceptualise being for what it really is, because it doesn't conform to its terms of reference. This is why we have to experience it to be truly able to appreciate it. This chapter concludes with a choiceless awareness practice for dropping into this experience.

Practice to try: Choiceless awareness

1. Find a place to sit, and begin with a period of mindfulness of breathing, followed by opening to mindfulness of body.

2. Expand to include sounds, smells, tastes and what you can see around you, allowing all of this to be experienced in awareness, moment by moment. Let sensory experience come to you, rather than going searching for it. Let any thoughts and evaluations be experienced in the same way, without chasing after or rejecting them. If there are physical or emotional reactions to what you are sensing, let these be felt with interest too, as events passing through consciousness just now.

3. There may be an awareness of moment-by-moment changes in experience, a sense of the ongoing, interconnected flow of what's happening in you and around you. Allow this too, but do not go looking for it or analyse it. Just open yourself to whatever is being experienced in the kindly space of awareness.

4. When you notice wandering into one particular aspect of experience, gently acknowledge this, then drop back into an equanimous appreciation of everything that is present.

5. As this choiceless awareness steadies, let go of any sense of practising a meditation 'technique'. Instead, rest in just being here and now, experiencing, noticing any clinging to or fighting against what is happening.

6. It can be helpful to re-ground the practice with mindfulness of breath or body, especially if you notice more distraction. Or simply be interested in the distraction and include it in your choiceless awareness each time you notice it.

7. Rest in choiceless awareness for as long as you like or have planned.

CHAPTER EIGHT

Rising up, Rooted …

If we surrendered to earth's intelligence,
we could rise up rooted, like trees.

Rainer Maria Rilke[1]

A t the last session of an eight-week mindfulness course, each participant is invited to describe what has changed for them.

'I've taken up gardening,' explains James, as he puts his hands on his hips in mock indignation. 'Now, I don't *do* gardening.'

Sally mentions, for the first time, that she gave up smoking after the third week. 'It was weird,' she says. 'I've been trying to quit for years, but after doing the body scan each day for a fortnight, I just stopped. It didn't feel right to do that to myself any more.'

Lauren's relationship with her family has shifted. 'At first, my daughter was upset that I was spending half an hour a day meditating upstairs. She said it was selfish. But for the first time in ages we've started talking properly again. Or rather, I've started listening, without judging or trying to change her. She seems to have responded to that. I get the sense she's starting to trust me again.'

These stories are typical of people who have begun to live their lives with mindfulness. More nourishing pursuits emerge, and they often find themselves acting more generously, with more tolerance, confidence and authenticity.

Bill was able to be present during a visit to a dying friend: 'He thanked me for being genuine with him, rather than trying to distract from what was happening.'

Josie stood up to colleagues at work, who were amazed by her assertiveness. 'I've always been the passive one, going along with the crowd. But there have been some changes in the office that I can't go along with, and I've got to speak up. If it makes no difference, then I'll find another job.'

Kamal hasn't attended the final class. It's his twenty-third birthday tonight, and he's celebrating with friends. 'I'll be sorry not to be there,' he said last week, 'but I haven't felt able to go out like this for ages. Just being in public made me crawl with anxiety. For the first time in a long time, I'm really looking forward to being with my mates.'

I've taught more than fifty of these courses, and it still amazes me to hear such stories. Partly I'm amused by what a slow learner I must be – it was years before I experienced the kinds of shifts that some people report after just a couple of months. But I'm also struck that these changes occur without our seeking them on the course. There are no modules on assertiveness at work, or how to handle a teenage daughter, or offering support to the terminally ill. And there are definitely no gardening sessions. All of the changes come organically from dropping into awareness, letting go of limiting beliefs and reactions, and learning simply to 'be' in a more gentle, abiding way. Everything else happens as a by-product.

What's going on here? How can it be that a practice that looks like inaction can lead to such transformations? And why is it so easy to get caught up in striving, struggling and straining for change when there's another, more organic option? A traditional image for meditation is of a rider on a horse. The rider appears to be deciding on the route, and may think he's in charge; but in order to become effective on horseback, he needs to listen to the animal that supports him. The horse knows intuitively how to navigate through the landscape, alive to cues from the environment, so is in a better position to take the lead. The rider may have an idea of the intended destination, but he is well advised to leave the basics of the journey to the horse, which can feel the best steps to take in each moment.

This ancient metaphor sits well with current research into the mind and body. While most of us automatically identify with thinking (the rider) and use it to control our path through life, experience is processed primarily in the body (the horse), which is powerfully in tune with reality on the ground. If we lose touch with this reality, disappearing into the disembodied doing mode of thought and frenzied action, that's like trying to make the horse a slave, tightening the reins to the point of cruelty. This does not make for a successful journey. We can't tune into what's happening all around, and the horse will be spooked by the rider's rough handling. Travelling like this, we are sure to be in for a bumpy ride.

As we practise mindfulness, rider and horse start to move in harmony. Recognising that the rider can trust the horse, we can choose to focus attention back in the body. We can still plan for the future, using the conceptual mode of mind, but by bringing awareness to the direct experience of the senses, we are able to tap into a power that thinking alone cannot access. With awareness, we become conscious of the whole scene.

None of this happens through struggle – the habitual human reaction to stress. All of the tools we need for mindfulness are already within us, so we don't need to fabricate them. Both the rider and the horse are available, and in good condition. We have the capacity to pay attention and to be aware of what's going on. We can be present to and interested in life, and we can learn from it. We *can* let go, and be gentle. So we just need to work well with what we have. Striving – including striving for mindfulness – tends to tangle us up, because it entails resistance to experiencing the moment. As soon as we try to escape to another state of mind, body or situation, we get in the way of the flow that comes when we are present. So we can let go of trying – or at least of trying hard. If there's any trying to be done, it should be soft – just a pointing and re-pointing of intention, attention and attitude towards whatever is happening. We can trust that whatever we are doing is likely to go better if we connect to it with mindfulness.

I didn't know any of this when I first suffered from depression. With my body behaving like a flailing, bucking bronco, my mind reacted like a rookie cowboy, battling in vain with his mount. It was only when I learned to meditate that another way presented itself. I stopped running from myself, and started to learn how to sit with experience. I began to tolerate small doses of reality, even when it hurt. Meditation held its mirror to an internal world I hadn't known how to view properly. I began to observe that thoughts and feelings were just aspects of that internal world; they didn't have to dominate my experience or control my behaviour. The more I was able to relate to the world from a space of awareness, the more I could permit difficulty to pass through. I didn't have to suppress, repress, attempt to avoid or wrestle with the challenges of difficult thoughts, feelings and events. In the allowing space of awareness, I learned that most of these dilemmas dissolved over time ... if I left them alone. And if action were necessary, I learned that it works best if it comes from awareness, rather than reaction.

This wasn't easy at first, maybe because I had suppressed or repressed so much over the years. With the unleashing of great hurricanes of emotion, propelling windmills of automatic thought, it was hard to stay present without being blown around. But as I began to trust and become more skilled at my practice, supported by an architecture of Buddhist teaching and more experienced meditators, even these tempests became more workable. Over time, their intensity diminished – perhaps because residual energy from the past had been released, perhaps because I was no longer creating and fighting against so many storms in the present. When the winds blew, I was more able to lean into them. Instead of feeling buffeted, I started to fly, like a kite.

I began to understand what was happening from new perspectives. As I learned that automatic reactions of thought and feeling are often based in bias – mind–body filters conditioned from the past – I found myself less caught up in them. I experienced with greater clarity how every aspect of life is in continual transition, and how everything is in an ongoing relationship with everything else, all of the time. Applying this view to the whole of life, I found a sense of place and purpose – a better understanding, certainly, but also some direction.

The spiritual teacher Nasargadatta Maharaj said: 'When I look inside and see that I am nothing, that's wisdom. When I look outside and see that I am everything, that's love. Between these two, my life turns.'[2] When we are able to recognise that there's no fixed self to experience from – but that we can experience whatever happens within and around us as part of a vast, flowing process of interconnection with the wider world – life starts to turn differently, without any help from us. A combination of a transformed view of and a transformed relationship with life naturally changes how we act. Harmony starts to happen, without any need for enforcement, hard work, resistance or suppression. Simply by being, our choices become wiser.

The best 'decisions' I've made in life weren't really made by 'me'. They were expressions of connection with existing energy in my mind, body and environment. Joining the community at Dechen Choling in 2006 made no sense from a conventional viewpoint. I swapped well-paid, flexible work for a volunteer role in a field with no career prospects. But I listened to my body, not my thoughts, and went anyway. Then, after I had 'decided' to stay at the retreat centre for the foreseeable future, my body told me to return to the UK, although I had no idea what I would do there. These two 'decisions' were pivotal in setting me on the most fulfilling, rewarding vocational path I could ever have imagined.

In February 2009, I began a new relationship. For the first time in my life, I felt a deep and calm sense of coherence with a partner, and within a few months I had asked her to marry me. Was this rapid move from first meeting to matrimony wise, from a rational point of view? With my relationship history, are you kidding? Yet it has turned out to be a partnership of great and happy steadiness, and it has produced two wonderful children. Like all partners, we have been through some challenges in our years together, but the profound and gentle resonance between us has proved sustaining. The connection we made was based on attunement, rather than craving or logic.

Resonances steer us when we make mindfulness a way of life. There are few prescriptions and no rules – a relationship or career choice that feels in tune for one person may feel dissonant for someone else. With our unique pasts contributing to the mind–body experience of life now, the choices we make will inevitably differ, too. However, if we can acknowledge and let go into the senses, allowing contemplation of and reflection on them gently to guide us, everything usually turns out well.

The cosmologist Brian Swimme has said that the most important scientific discovery so far is that hydrogen gas turns into rose bushes, giraffes and human beings if left alone for fourteen billion years.[3] This serves as a good reminder for practice. Much of life is inexplicable, but if we can be in the flow as part of a process of the world unfolding, then we are in the best position to live well – attuning to things as much as we can, influencing them sometimes, but controlling them almost never.

It's difficult to comprehend this. Human domination of our planet has come from our capacity to conceptualise, with reasoning used as a tool to manipulate the world around us. But the cost of ignoring direct experience – of disconnecting from the senses – is a loss of communion with the flow of nature. Rather than recognising and celebrating the thinking mind as the rider who works with the horse of experience, we imagine that the rider can also play the horse's role, forgetting that we are deeply dependent on the powerful animal within us. Our culture supports the coronation of rider as king, as we all pretend that every minor triumph of intellectual prowess indicates that we can achieve almost anything we want, and eradicate almost anything we don't want. Meanwhile, the realities of life and death continue to stare us in the face.

From the perspective of the doing mode, mindfulness meditation might seem rather passive. But this couldn't be further from the truth. Being in the flow actually requires wholehearted engagement with whatever is happening. Accepting where we are right now, we may come to see and feel that some action is needed to co-create the future. But it's only through connecting with this moment as it is (rather than trying – or pretending – to like it, resisting it or ignoring it) that we help to create a synchrony that enables wise, embodied action. Acceptance doesn't mean inactivity; it means letting your movement come from your deepest being, in tune with the world as you find it. When we act with presence, whatever we do is likely to go better, without any attempt to *make* that happen.

Victor Frankl, the author of *Man's Search for Meaning*, articulated this when he urged his readers not to aim for success: 'The more you aim at it and make it a target, the more you are going to miss it,' he wrote. 'Success cannot be pursued; it must ensue, and it only does so as the unintended side-effect of one's personal dedication to a cause greater than oneself.' Similarly, 'Happiness must happen, and you have to let it happen by not caring about it.' This all sounds rather counter-intuitive – we are more likely to achieve what we want by not trying to achieve it. Yet Frankl's message was clear: 'I want you to listen to what your conscience commands you to do and go on to carry it out to the best of your knowledge. Then you will live to see that in the long run – in the long run, I say! – success will follow you precisely because you had forgotten to think about it.'[4]. As Lao Tzu famously summarised: 'Search your heart and see/the way to do is to be.'[5]

This is the way of mindfulness. Working on the mind and body that perceive and act on events, rather than on the events themselves, it can seem like nothing much is happening when we meditate. But in transforming the apparatus of consciousness, meditation changes how we see, connect and act on everything that happens. And when we continue to follow this approach outside of our formal mindfulness practice, it becomes a simple and effective way of life. Rather than trying to change the world with a scattered, frantic, deluded mind, we settle and free that mind, then let it change the world through an enlightened meeting with it.

At the beginning of a mindfulness course, participants may be asked to outline changes they'd like to see in their lives as a result of the programme. The answers come tumbling out: better sleep, more happiness, less pain, greater presence, improved connection with others, better relationships with work colleagues, calmness, protection from depression or worry, less tendency to get stuck in the past or the future, increased control, and so on. After acknowl-edging the wisdom of these goals, the teacher will suggest that each student should let go of trying to achieve any of them. Instead, they are invited just to give themselves over to following the curriculum for the duration of the programme. The teacher will invite the students to practise mindfulness – that's all.

This invitation usually evokes surprise and relief in equal measure. Surprise, because abandoning goals runs counter to how we
expect to get on in this world; and relief, perhaps because something deep within us knows that the struggle to be a better, a
happier or even a more mindful person is doomed to failure, as
it will only perpetuate a mode of mind that is unable to rest in
contentment. Mindfulness teaches us to let the moment be whatever it is, and to meet it with kindly awareness. As it happens, this
often leads to good outcomes, because when we meet the moment
in this way, we stop getting in the way. By contrast, as soon as we
struggle to escape what is here, we move into a conceptually driven
desire for a prescribed future, which virtually guarantees that the
approach will fail.

In one study, new graduates were asked how often they 'experienced positive thoughts, images, or fantasies on the subject of
transition into work life, graduating from university, looking for
and finding a job'. Two years down the line, the graduates who had
expressed the most positive thoughts about the future had sent off
the fewest job applications, received the fewest offers of work and
were earning the lowest salaries. Research has also found that hip-
surgery patients who fantasised about walking without pain tend
to take longer to recover.[6] When we get caught up in projections
and reactions, we block happiness and success. These are the 'ironic
processes' that the psychologist Daniel Wegner studied.[7]

Buddhist teachings have described this phenomenon for thousands of years. In one vivid image, we are propelled around the
cogs of the wheel of suffering (samsara) by a chain of unfortunate
attitudes and reactions. We go from delusion to craving to impulsive activity and worsening circumstances, the stress of which
embeds our delusion even further. Round and round we go on
the wheel, with the grooves that keep us stuck deepening all the
time. However, there's one link in the chain where the cycle can

be stopped. In the moment of direct contact with each event in our life, change can come if we meet it with awareness. If we can watch our reactivity arise, we are no longer bound to follow it. With awareness, we have another option.

The more we train attention and a compassionate, steadfast presence, the more we can refrain from impulsive reaction. Rather than being tied to the spinning wheel of *samsara*, we are more able to affect the course of our life. Although our conditioning operates powerfully – from the very composition of our body, mind and world to the habits we have adopted from family, friends and our wider culture – we can gently work towards freedom. However, this can come only when we drop the struggle for success that creates more stress, and put our energy into relating to whatever's happening now. As soon as we let go of the battle to reach our goals we establish the conditions for change, because battling itself is the key impediment to achieving those goals.

I like to describe processes simply, and I often explain mindfulness as an 'ABC' skill. The more we are aware (A), and can skilfully be (B), the more our range of choice (C) expands. With awareness, we start to discern what will help in each situation. Refraining from automatic reaction, there's some space to test out new actions, the results of which we can observe with curiosity. As with any behaviour, simply carrying out the action strengthens a pattern within our consciousness, making it easier to perform the next time. With awareness, we can see and feel whether what we did was useful, which provides further feedback to guide our next decisions, when the time comes to make them. By bringing mindfulness to life like this on an ongoing basis, we are like a scientist observing the results of a series of experiments and a craftsman honing a skill, training ourselves to handle each moment deftly. With this scientist–craftsman approach, we find the understanding and the resources to live life well. We start to know what to do without any need for a specific set of instructions for every situation. Bringing our wise mind to each unfolding event, we know and feel how to act intuitively.

It helps to take a long view of this transformation. For while mindfulness invites us to act from our hearts, history and habits make this difficult. In the rush of doing and the fog of thinking, we easily lose touch. Rather than decisions flowing organically, based on a clear, unclinging connection with the world, we get stuck in our ideas, opinions and old habits, which wrench us from embodied wisdom. We become disintegrated, befuddled, fragmented, confused.

A virtue of the Buddhist image of *samsara* and the work of liberation is that they encourage patience. It is said that the dissolution of destructive habits takes place over an almost infinite number of epochs known as *kalpas*. One *kalpa* is the length of time it takes for an eagle to wear the highest mountain down to the ground, by brushing a silk handkerchief over the summit each time it flies past on its way around the world. Understood like this, we can abandon our habitual grasping for quick fixes and our patterns of self-judgement when we fail to 'measure up'. This is good, because self-judgement gets in the way and quick fixes never last – our grasping for them reinforces patterns of craving.

Nevertheless, *some* effort is required. Paradoxically, in order to let go into attuned, spontaneous action, we must practise the method of mindfulness, because this helps us to let go. It is important to note the difference here between following intentions and chasing goals. If we didn't follow the intention to meditate, we would never begin our practice. But whereas a goal is an imaginary, external target, fixed in the future, an intention describes what's within us right now. Generating, connecting with and following an intention means repeatedly choosing a path that starts wherever we are. It can be followed with steadfastness, but it is also flexible, changing in the light of circumstances.

Intentions are generated and followed by connecting with experience in the body. Because the five senses can attune only to what's happening in the moment, attachment to concept-based, goal-oriented thinking falls away when we offer our soft, sustained attention to sensations. Actions inspired by this connection are more likely to be congruent, because they are in touch with what's happening, more so than ideas and opinions. Free from projected or desired outcomes, yet willing to be moved by the winds of experience, we can become deeply authentic in our responses. This was what Victor Frankl meant by 'listening to your conscience'. We tune into the longings of the heart and let them guide us along and fuel our journey.

Most of us need guidance from experienced others, too – teachers to point out our blind spots, and a community of peers for mutual support. Meditation practice is an excellent way of cultivating mindfulness, but unless we engage with people who can help us attune to the world, the effect will probably be limited. Especially in the early years of my practice, I benefited greatly from the strong reinforcement of Buddhist principles and practice provided by the intentional communities at the London Shambhala Meditation Centre and Dechen Choling. I'm deeply grateful for their gentle (and sometimes fierce) support of my practice, their willingness to tolerate my distress, and their patient guidance. Without their help, I doubt I would have been able to stay present to the storms that arose within me.

It's helpful to follow a clear, comprehensive and well-trodden path. The Buddhist tradition describes eight aspects of the training that leads to freedom. These include clearly seeing one's predicament ('right view') and choosing to orient one's life from that perspective ('right intention'). One's approach to being in the world follows from these, by making commitments to 'right speech', 'right action', 'right effort' and 'right livelihood'. We can also work to transform the mind through 'right mindfulness' and 'right concentration'. These should not be viewed as dictates of a moral code, but more like a medical treatment plan, based on the recognition that certain ways of relating and behaving tend to lead to more favourable outcomes. When we stray from the plan, we are invited to observe what happened and use this as a basis for further learning, rather than descend into self-recrimination. It helps to view the word 'right' in each aspect not in terms of morality, but as wise and likely to lead to happiness, rather than unwise and likely to lead to unhappiness.

I'm also guided these days by a network of supervisors, fellow teachers, and course participants, as well as a body of research and other studies, based on the methods of mainstream mindfulness. These act as further reminders to return to presence when my intentions, attention and actions become disconnected. I'm learning too from the evidence base that continues to grow in the science of well-being. This tells us, for example, that practising gratitude is demonstrably beneficial – people who keep a 'gratitude journal' each day are happier, healthier and more resilient, even when they find themselves in difficult circumstances.[8] Generosity is similarly advantageous, bringing rewards to the recipient *and* the donor. In one study, people reported feeling happier when they spent money on others rather than themselves, even when they had not expected this to be the case.[9] On the other hand, those who take a materialistic approach to life tend to be less happy – they experience fewer positive emotions and they are more prone to anxiety, depression and substance abuse.[10] More than ever before, we have access to a vast range of techniques – honed over millennia – that can guide us to more competent living. Tried and tested in people's lives – as well as through scientific enquiry – they can help us too, if we put them into practice.

But we can't do this alone. In a culture that promotes the delusion of individualism, many of us believe we have sole responsibility for our lives. Mindfulness training shows us that this isn't the case. We are deeply connected to and affected by others. Of course, we can practise with our own mind and body to heal ourselves from within, but the liberation will be limited unless we are also tuned to the wider world. The more we can create and connect with structures in life that engender wise choices, not just for ourselves but for everyone else, the happier we are likely to be. The Dalai Lama has described this as a kind of selfish altruism – the best way for each of us to be happy is to work alongside others and offer ourselves in service to community.[11] Many studies have shown that those who have strong social connections tend to be happier and healthier than those who don't. Indeed, some researchers have suggested that loneliness may cause more physical harm than obesity or smoking.[12]

With connection comes kindness. As we get closer to others, compassion (literally 'feeling with') becomes not just a logical choice or an ethical imperative but a living, felt sense. We start to appreciate the wisdom of John Watson's words: 'Be kind, for everyone you meet is carrying a heavy burden.'[13] Compassion comes naturally from mindfulness practice. From the very beginning, with the soft reminder to return to the breath or the body when we notice the mind wandering, the approach invites gentleness. Again and again, we practise letting go of harsh judgements. As we recognise the force of our own habits, we begin to realise that others are ensnared by their automatic reactions, too. By meeting our own difficulties, we become aware of the challenges that every human faces. Realising that the walls we erect between us aren't so solid – and that the interconnections in our lives can be fostered – we start to feel closer to others. We are all together in this marvellous, mysterious universe – one enormous, extended family.

My most difficult times were spent in self-imposed solitary confinement. I built a world in which I lived alone and worked alone. I was fearful of exposing my internal world to others, so I stayed well away from them. Even when I was in company, I erected rigid psychic barriers that sealed me in isolation. I tried to relate to others in support groups and therapy, but the thick barriers made interaction almost impossible. It was only when I discovered a community of meditators, who accepted me in a way that was not infantilising, that I began to experience genuine mutual support. As I felt more able to let myself be known, no longer fearing rejection, I started to relax. And the more relaxed I became, the better I felt, and the more I was able to give.

This is a gradual process for most of us. My tendency is still to isolate, especially when I feel overwhelmed. But the more I've practised, especially with others, the more comfortable I've felt within relationships. These days I benefit from a range of feedback loops that support and sustain my connections. I'm more in touch with my parents, who are now the grandparents of our two children, and being part of an extended family draws me into loving contact many times each day. I'm also connected in our local community, meeting many people who are involved in our boys' care and education, as well as neighbours and others at social events and parties.

Moreover, I feel deeply connected to the practice that has helped me so much, and it's a joy to share it with others. Having found a vocation that inspires me, I'm lucky enough to work with groups of people who are exploring presence in their own lives. I hear of their struggles, stories and shifts, and I'm privileged to walk with them on part of their journey. When their breakthroughs come, they often remind me of my own. The glowing resonance of our connection warms my heart, as it seems to warm theirs. The more everyone gives to everyone else, acting from a sense of compassion and care, the better we all feel. In giving ourselves repeatedly to presence, connection and love, through the mindfulness practices we learn and the supports for awareness we create, life becomes more oriented in the direction of sanity. This should come as no surprise, because sanity is the expression of awareness – present, connected and kind. These qualities are cultivated and nourished by practising mindfulness, and then they seep into the world around us.

Life can change through exposure to mindfulness – through the gentle, intentional training and by staying in touch with mindful people and structures. With a mind inclined to kindly awareness, we meet each circumstance more fully and skilfully. We make better choices, and the structures we build around us and the relationships we make become expressions of compassionate consciousness. This leads to greater contentment for ourselves – and for everyone else in our lives. As we burden them less, they are more inclined to bring wisdom and kindness to their own situations. And so it goes around – a virtuous loop of wise, present-centred relationships that eventually becomes more powerful as the driver of our lives, replacing the old automatic habits and reactions that used to drag us into stress.

Uncovering compassion

Looking after oneself, one looks after others.
Looking after others, one looks after oneself.
And how does one look after others by looking after oneself? By practising [mindfulness], by developing [it], by doing [it] a lot.

The Buddha[14]

In an ingenious experiment, Paul Condon and his colleagues demonstrated that consideration for others emerges naturally from mindfulness training.[15] The researchers invited a group of people who had taken an eight-week course (as well as a control group who had not) to their laboratory at Northeastern University in the United States, ostensibly to measure their brain activity. However, the real experiment involved observing what happened in the crowded waiting room outside the lab. As each person waited to be called in, a woman would enter the room on crutches, visibly wincing. With no seats available, she would sigh and lean against a wall.

The supposedly injured lady was actually an actor working for the researchers, and several of those seated in the waiting room were stooges as well – their instructions were to ignore the woman on crutches. This was meant to induce the so-called 'bystander effect' – whereby people are less likely to help when those around them fail to leap into action. However, those who had taken the mindfulness course were more than five times as likely to offer the woman their seat, compared to those who hadn't attended the programme.

Why did the mindfulness-trained participants respond in this way? There are many possible explanations, but they were probably more attentive to the situation in front of them, more attuned to the likely distress of the woman on crutches, and less conditioned by the inaction of others in the waiting room. Reduced stress was probably a factor, too. An earlier experiment revealed that when a group of students were late for an appointment (some of them on their way to a lecture on the story of the Good

Samaritan!), 90 per cent of them rushed past a person slumped by the side of the road. A majority of another group who believed they had plenty of time (and were therefore less likely to feel stressed) stopped to help the injured person.[16]

The predominant view in our culture is that everyone is naturally competitive, but an increasing body of evidence suggests that, in many circumstances, our spontaneous first response is actually to help others. (This is true even of small children, who have yet to learn social conventions relating to kindness.)[17] While there's no doubt that competing is common, could it be that aggressive actions are primarily conditioned as automatic reactions to perceived threats and stress? When we feel more at peace, more compassionate responses emerge from within, perhaps as a consequence of our increased well-being. We relax, open up and connect.

This would explain why people trained in mindfulness – which is known to reduce stress and increase well-being – tend to act compassionately even when they have not trained specifically in showing kindness to others. Given that many studies also suggest that acting with kindness is good for our own health and happiness,[18] there may be a mutual connecting of the feedback loops that link mindfulness, kindness and well-being. The more mindful we are, the better we feel and the kinder we are; and the better we feel and the kinder we are, the more mindful we will be.

Practice to try: Listening to the horse

Mindfulness trains us to 'listen to the horse' – the intuitive sense of feeling in the body. If we can let go of overthinking and overreacting, the patterns handed down to us through evolution seem quite well adapted for guiding us through the world. They can help us make good decisions if we can connect to them. This doesn't mean ignoring the thinking mind – we still need it to formulate our intentions, to interpret the sensations we experience, and to decide how to respond to them. But thinking often works best in the service of experience, rather than the other way around. This 'horse-whispering' practice, based on the breathing space meditation that is used in the MBCT course, promotes connection with wisdom in the body, especially when we are unsure of what – if anything – we need to do in a given situation.

1. Drop into the being mode – adopt a comfortable seated posture, become still, and turn attention to what is going on in your mind and body right now. Connect with awareness by noticing the thoughts and sensations that are present. Acknowledge them, but do not do anything else with them. Rest in observation for a few moments.

2. Bring a gentle focus to breathing in the belly, following its rhythm for a while. Allow the mind to settle into the breath, with everything else allowed in the background.

3. Expanding to a wider focus, open up to all sensations in the body, without preference for any of them. Experience pleasant, unpleasant and neutral sensations alike with

a friendly awareness, watching and experiencing their movement within.

4. Now, ask a question about some aspect of your life. It could be a choice you have to make, a difficulty you face, or a wider issue relating to your purpose or direction. It might be as simple as: 'Is there anything I need to do right now?' or 'How can I be of help today?' Or it might be as profound as: 'What do I intend to do with the rest of my life?' Let the question drop into your heart and body, and listen to any answers that arise from there. The answers may appear as words in the mind, or they may be felt as body sensations. Attend to them carefully, without seeking specific answers. Notice when the thinking mind tries to come up with answers, which may tend to carry a more frantic energy. See if you can trust what comes from your 'wise mind', even if it's nothing or not what you expected. Remember, you don't have to *do* anything. What you experience (even if it's nothing) is information for you to tune into, no more or less. Sometimes, the best action is no action.

5. Let go of the question, and any answers that have arisen. Return to mindfulness of the breath for a while.

You can practise this meditation at any time. However, it's usually more helpful if you have spent some time on the longer, foundational practices such as mindfulness of breath, body and the body scan, all of which are oriented to connecting with sensation, in awareness.

CHAPTER NINE

And Collectively ...

Interest in mindfulness within the mainstream
of society and its institutions is rapidly
becoming a global phenomenon, supported
by increasingly rigorous scientific research, and
driven in part by a longing for new models
and practices that might help us individually
and collectively to apprehend and solve the
challenges threatening our health as societies
and as a species, optimizing the preconditions
for happiness and well-being, and minimizing
the causes and pre-conditions for
unhappiness and suffering.

Jon Kabat-Zinn[1]

While I was working on the Mental Health Foundation's
mindfulness report in 2009, I was also drafting chapters
for a book called *The Mindful Manifesto*, co-authored with a doctor in
general practice, Jonty Heaversedge. The book was meant to serve
as an introduction to mindfulness for individuals, but it also suggested that the approach might be valuable for working with some
of society's difficulties, by promoting more widespread health and
well-being. In the opening chapter, we asked readers to imagine

what it would be like to live in a world where mindfulness courses were widely available to the general population, where the practices were taught to schoolchildren, and where the approach was given regular coverage in the mainstream media. Half-jokingly, we wondered what might happen if politicians 'sat mindfully in meditation for 10 minutes before each session of Parliament, pausing to disengage their egos and notice how unhelpful old patterns of thought and feelings might be driving their decisions'.[2]

Although mindfulness training was becoming increasingly common at this time, with a few National Health Service trusts offering courses, Jonty and I didn't expect what we described to become reality. Yet, over the next few years, mindfulness exploded into the public domain. Courses *are* now widely available, and mindfulness training seems to be everywhere – from aeroplane in-flight channels to business school MBA programmes. Healthcare professionals regularly recommend it to their patients, and there has been a steady expansion of mindfulness courses offered in NHS settings. Mindfulness gets mentioned in TV soap operas, and, as I write, the Barbican Theatre in London is about to present the world's first 'mindfulness opera'. Thousands of articles have been written about the approach in newspapers and magazines.

This revolution, as well as its rapidity, is astonishing. A few years ago, meditation was widely perceived as an inherently counter-cultural practice by a world that worshipped doing, go-getting, grasping and achieving. Yet now here it is, taking centre stage in a vibrant discourse on how to live more happily and sanely.

Troubled by the suffering in life, and by the apparent lack of options for working with it, many people have been drawn to an approach that addresses the root causes of stress. Most of us realise that the world isn't in a good state, and that the manner in which we interact is often unskilful. We would like to follow a different path, and mindfulness practice makes intuitive sense to many of those who encounter it. We know in our hearts that patterns of craving and aversion lead to behaviour that creates misery, and that an approach promoting stillness, gentleness, authenticity and steadfastness will likely be beneficial.

Mindfulness has permeated into the mainstream of public life partly because the training has become more socially acceptable. It is now viewed – correctly – as a non-religious, scientifically researched way of working with challenges in a stressful world. Jon Kabat-Zinn took the core teachings of the Buddhist tradition and presented them in a way that resonates with non-Buddhist cultures, as practical ways of working with modern life's difficulties. Most of us understand and feel the pressures of constant demands for attention, pulling our minds from one device to the next in a ceaseless whirlpool of activity. One estimate suggests that consumption of information in the Western world has increased by 350 per cent over the last three decades.[3] Our brains aren't wired to cope with this onslaught, irrespective of how much we try to multitask, and we know and feel the effects.

By helping people make the choice just to be – in silence and stillness – for perhaps no more than a few minutes each day, mindfulness practice helps us develop the strength and skill to cultivate well-being in a culture whose influence is often damaging to it. Simultaneously, it trains us to work with our experience as it arises, in a way that helps us manage the rest of life when we are not engaged in formal meditation. This is desperately needed. In just one snapshot of the world's growing unhappiness, the World Health Organisation predicts that depression will be the most burdensome illness on the planet by the year 2030.[4]

Importantly, scientists have continued to develop a robust and varied evidence base for mindfulness. Since 2009, when I first reviewed this evidence for the Mental Health Foundation, thousands more papers have explored the effects of mindfulness courses, and more than five hundred peer-reviewed journal articles on the subject are now being published each year. Many of these point to the value of the practice in numerous fields and aspects of life.

In the realm of healthcare, a meta-analysis of trials involving more than twelve thousand people found 'large and clinically significant effects in treating anxiety and depression, and the gains were maintained at follow-up'.[5] According to the research, people who are prone to depression seem to benefit most. Our likelihood of relapsing once we have experienced several episodes of depression is greatly reduced by attending a course of mindfulness-based cognitive therapy; a meta-analysis of six high-quality trials in this area found an average 44 per cent reduction in relapse rates.[6] Trials of mindfulness training for people with physical health problems have also achieved promising results – people with conditions ranging from cancer and cardiovascular disease to diabetes and chronic pain seem to respond well. The practice has helped numerous substance abusers, too.[7]

Other benefits of mindfulness training include reduced reactivity to emotionally charged stimuli, improved cognitive performance and mental flexibility, better immune system functioning, improved sleep, more satisfying relationships, and less loneliness.[8] People trained in mindfulness are also more likely to engage in pro-social and environmentally friendly behaviour,[9] and they tend to feel a greater sense of inner peace.[10]

In the workplace, mindfulness-trained people have been shown to be more able to manage the demands of a busy office environment – their mood is more resilient and they are more able to stay on task.[11] Other studies have suggested that job performance improves among people who have taken a mindfulness course. For instance, school teachers report feeling less stress and greater capacity to manage their thoughts and actions. They are also more likely to relate with empathy, patience and tolerance, and exhibit better coping skills, teaching ability, motivation, planning and problem-solving.[12] Meanwhile, doctors trained in mindfulness are less likely to experience burnout, connect better with and have more time for their patients, and provide a higher quality of care.[13]

There is mounting evidence that children and young people benefit from mindfulness training. They are less likely to suffer from stress, anxiety and depression, and report improvements in general well-being, emotion and behaviour regulation, as well as self-esteem and sleep quality. Objective measures of attention and academic performance show marked improvements, too. As with adults, mindfulness appears to help children form constructive social relationships, as well as cope with the inevitable difficulties of life. Similarly, mindful parenting programmes seem to reduce parental stress and destructive behaviour while improving emotional availability. Unsurprisingly, this has a positive impact on the behaviour of the children, too.[14]

The emergence of this scientific evidence base, together with more culturally accepted forms for transmitting the practice, has enabled mindfulness to blossom in public life, including in the world of politics. In 2012, Chris Ruane, who at the time was the Member of Parliament for the Vale of Clwyd, made a speech in the House of Commons. The debate was on unemployment, and Chris advocated the use of mindfulness courses to help people cope with the difficulties of being out of work. Later, I met him to discuss his vision for a mindful political culture, which was both more developed and less tentative than the one that Jonty and I had proposed in *The Mindful Manifesto*. More to the point, Chris was a politician, so he had the experience and the connections to make his ideas reality.

First, he explained, MPs had to be introduced to the method. He knew that it would be unwise for them to recommend mindfulness-based policies without engaging with the practice themselves. He had therefore arranged for Chris Cullen, a teacher at the Oxford University Mindfulness Centre, to give weekly classes in Parliament. All 650 MPs were invited to attend, as well as members of the House of Lords. Over the next two years, more than a hundred parliamentarians accepted the invitation, as did some of their staff, and a core of mindfulness-trained politicians was established at Westminster.

Having laid the groundwork, Chris Ruane and several colleagues set up the Mindfulness All-Party Parliamentary Group (MAPPG) to explore the potential for fostering mindfulness in public life. Just prior to the launch of the MAPPG, I was contacted by Madeleine Bunting, then a senior editor at the *Guardian* newspaper, who had co-founded an advocacy group with Chris Cullen to support the MPs in their work. Over the next year, I worked with Madeleine as co-director of the Mindfulness Initiative, which helped the MAPPG launch an inquiry into the role that mindfulness might play in government and politics. Together with dozens of associates and advisers drawn from a variety of disciplines, we held hearings in Parliament on mindfulness in healthcare, education, the workplace and the criminal justice system, in which experts from each field offered their knowledge, experience and advice.

The inquiry's findings were eventually crystallised into a report titled *Mindful Nation UK*. This made a range of recommendations, calling for more funding for mindfulness-based approaches in healthcare, the development of mindfulness training in education, and the provision of courses for government and other public sector staff.[15] It emphasises that mindfulness is beneficial not just for people who are unwell but for most people, because it cultivates well-being and resilience. According to the executive summary:

Mindfulness has a role to play in tackling our mental health crisis, in which roughly one in three families include someone who is mentally ill ... Equally importantly, we need to take prevention strategies seriously, if we are to reduce the burden of mental ill health, and encourage the flourishing and well-being of a healthy nation. Mindfulness is one of the most promising prevention strategies and is regarded as popular and non-stigmatising.[16]

The fruits of the inquiry and report will take time to ripen, but, if nothing else, their very existence is remarkable. When politicians show a willingness to take mindfulness seriously, the communities that elect them are more likely to do the same.

Some politicians have revealed that the approach has helped them in their own frantic lives. For instance, Tracey Crouch, the first Conservative co-chair of the MAPPG and now Minister for Sport and the Olympics, explained that mindfulness helped her cope when she was depressed. 'At first I was sceptical,' she said. 'I thought it was an airy-fairy type of thing. But I completely changed my view ... The mindfulness course helped me develop coping mechanisms, and to understand the mind ... It has also helped build my confidence in vulnerable situations, like speaking on live radio or in the House of Commons.'[17] Similarly, Lorely Burt, a Liberal Democrat and another co-chair of the group, said: 'In the past I have experienced depression and so I know what it's like when it's creeping back up ... Since using the mindfulness exercises, I have been more cogent in my thinking, more confident in speaking up. It's helped me to find the confidence to put myself forward and deal with that self-criticism which can hold you back. I enjoy my life more.'[18]

As those who have felt the benefits of mindfulness in their own lives continue to express and share their experiences with others, a movement is emerging. Mindfulness projects have been launched in numerous organisations and institutions, usually led by people who have trained in the practice themselves, and have been inspired to share it with others. When introduced skilfully, there can be a mindfulness ripple effect through whole communities, extending out to every member. As the word and the practice have spread, meditation has been introduced to and by schoolteachers, health professionals, police officers, lawyers, aid workers, journalists (in both new and traditional media) and technology specialists, as well as in many other professional and social settings.

Mindfulness is more than a self-help phenomenon. While the practice may seem to be something that is done by and for individuals, through it we eventually realise that there is no purely personal world, experience or behaviour. When we recognise that experience is conditioned by processes that come from both outside and inside ourselves, we can no longer maintain an artificial separation between these aspects of living. What happens within us affects what happens around us; and what happens around us affects what happens within us. We are products of our biology and our psychology, for sure, but also of our history, society, economic system and wider culture. Reciprocally, these collective aspects of life comprise what we bring to them as groups of connected individuals.

As mindfulness opens us up, we learn to notice how we are affected by the world, and how we affect it. Letting ourselves be touched by this connection, with the barriers down, tends to be a moving experience. Feeling the difficulties of those around us, we resonate with them. Without any attempt to try to be good, or to follow a set of externally imposed ethics, people who practise mindfulness often report a spontaneous inspiration to help others. Our hearts naturally fill with compassion. We know we can make a difference. So, as we feel the intimacy of our connection to others and the world, we reach out and offer what we can. The less stressed we feel – perhaps as a result of our meditation practice – the more we open up rather than close down, and the more adept our help becomes, with mindfulness as our foundation. This is the beginning of a broader, more socially oriented mindfulness. In the Buddhist traditions, it is the realisation of the bodhisattva, the name given to someone who recognises that their own full awakening from the patterns that perpetuate anguish can come about only by encouraging that same awakening in all beings.

How might this manifest itself, and when? As with any other aspect of the practice, there are no set rules. We can be guided by our hearts, minds and opportunities that arise. Some of us are inspired to follow a more compassionate career. Others may volunteer to help people in need. Others may care for children or older people, and bring their practice to this endeavour. Still others may become political activists and advocate for societal change. Every expression of mindfulness makes a difference. The good news, according James Fowler and Nicholas Christakis, is that when one person becomes happier and healthier, those around them become healthier and happier, too.[19]

We don't need to be driven by guilt or anger, or force ourselves into something for which we are unprepared. For some, their meditation practice may continue to be their act of service – just by taking the time to stop, be still and look inward, we engage with one of the most radical and transformative acts imaginable, because we refrain from fuelling the treadmill of culturally sanctioned craving. It's normal and advisable first to focus on developing a personal practice, observing and learning to work with patterns of reaction in our own experience. We can then experiment with bringing our mindfulness into close relationships, opening up with patience and love in our connections with friends and family. Whatever form our service takes, we can know that each act that comes from mindful awareness is a gift to others, ourselves and the world.

Society's problems are the mind's problems writ large. The

materialistic worldview that values production, consumption and profit for their own sake is an external manifestation of the grasping, delusion and fear that dominate the human mind. Such is the human drive to acquire and plunder that we have put ourselves at grave risk of rendering our planet uninhabitable. Yet, the more we continue to experience ourselves as separated from everything and everyone around us, the more we are likely to feel impelled to cling to and crave 'possessions', whether these are in the form of ideologies, territories or material goods. Unconsciously, when I started practising, my patterns of relating to the world were largely based on the notion of material transaction. What can I get from this person, thing or experience? How I reacted to everything and everyone around me was based on this materialistic worldview – I would try to reject whoever or whatever I thought was unable to increase my level of contentment, grasping instead at whoever or whatever I felt might bring me happiness. I had little sense of the public sphere, of the wider community, or of the importance of connecting with and contributing something positive to the world. It was a selfish existence, and a discontented one. My recovery began when I started to let go of this fixation on making things better for myself and instead cultivated a gentler, more flexible, more allowing connection, first with my own mind, then with everything with which it came into contact. It was no coincidence that I began to feel better when I started to let go in my inner world – and into healthier, more mutually supportive relationships.

In its capacity to help us bring attention to experience, courage to presence and skill to behaviour, mindfulness sets us firmly on the path to change. Simultaneously, every change we make in ourselves is also a change in the world. The more we are able to transform our own lives and cultivate greater well-being, the more the environment benefits. Every time we notice and unhook from our patterns of clinging and aggression, and instead choose a response that springs from a place of embodied presence, we are cooling the flames of craving and aggression that burn through our planet.

If we can also work collectively to spread mindfulness through our environment, then we generate energy for an even deeper transformation. This is why the expansion of meditation training into public life could be so valuable. Rather than helping individuals cope within dysfunctional environments, as is sometimes suggested, mindfulness, if practised collectively, could usher in a new kind of culture. If enough of us continue to practise – offering our practice to relationships at home, at work, and elsewhere – then all of these places can gradually be transformed from generators of stress to places of peace. If this happens, our world will be more nurturing for those who grow up and live within it. In turn, this would to lead to greater overall happiness and less stress, and the prospect of even deeper mindfulness. Hence the positive mutual feedback loop could continue to reinforce itself – with people transforming communities, and communities transforming people.

An intriguing study of mindfulness in the workplace suggests this process is already under way.[20] In the trial, a group of managers received mindfulness training, but the effects were observed among those who worked for them. These employees experienced less emotional exhaustion, had better work–life balances, and achieved higher performance ratings. They were also more likely to show concern for their co-workers and express their opinions honestly. Their managers' practice – and perhaps the effect it had on how they led their teams – apparently had a significant impact on the employees' well-being and behaviour, even though those employees had not received mindfulness training themselves. If something similar is happening in other environments where people are practising, then we may already be on our way to happier homes, schools and communities.

We must ensure our enthusiasm for mindfulness doesn't turn into a grasping or aggressive campaign. We could get so carried away by our desire to change the world, or spread the message of mindfulness, that the message itself and the manner of its delivery will cease to be mindful. As soon as we find ourselves preaching, or pushing people into a course, we will have moved into separation and solidification, closing ourselves off from connection, rather than remaining curious and open. We are likely to win hearts and minds only by listening to, understanding and exploring the opinions of those who disagree with us.

A mindful society will emerge only if we are prepared to engage mindfully with the world as it is. As the Buddhist teacher Pema Chödrön reminds us, we have to 'start where we are'.[21] This means finding ways to connect with people in the midst of their lives, with their current stresses, in their current environments. It means inviting mindful leadership, and mindful collective action, working within the systems, organisations and cultures of our society, in a way that can guide us to sanity. And it means protecting the integrity of the approach, guarding it against the subtle and not-so-subtle perversions that could render it ineffective. We should keep coming back to the core attitudes, practices and principles of the training – such as turning towards difficulty, non-fixation, presence and patience – so that mindfulness is not presented as passivity, selfishness, ideology or a quick fix.

Chris Ruane's approach to bringing mindfulness into politics serves as a good model. By inviting fellow politicians to experience the practice for themselves, he encouraged an understanding and embodiment of mindfulness among his colleagues prior to making policy suggestions. Some of the politicians who have taken the mindfulness course at Westminster have said the programme gave them a rare opportunity to dismantle barriers and speak intimately in the presence of 'the opposition'. Might this be the start of a more mindful political sphere? If so, it could be just as important as the politicians' proposals to encourage mindfulness in other institutions and services.

So many aspects of our political culture seem to be entrenched in the kinds of aggression and evasion that preclude contentment, connection and inclusive, community-centred action. The frenzied pursuit of ever more influence, the fear of rejection and criticism, the frantic pressure to act (or at least to give the impression of acting), and the adversarial party-based system that divides everyone into one camp or the other are all manifestations of the 'right-or-wrong' fixation that dominates the world. We all contribute to this with our casual opinions about what our political leaders ought to achieve, and we judge their actions coldly, marking crosses every so often on pieces of paper. In such a culture, it's difficult to remain connected to awareness and compassion.

I've often visited the Houses of Parliament in my work with the MAPPG, and I invariably leave with a headache. There's the frequent, piercing clang of the division bell, calling MPs to vote, but also a more general frenzy that seems to create and concentrate the pain in my temples. Feeling this pain makes it easier for me to connect with the challenges that the politicians face. If just a day in Parliament gives me a headache, what must it do to those who work there every day? Hearing MPs speak about the pressures of the job – the constant demands for attention, the stark judgements made of them and the innumerable responsibilities – has led me to view the political process, and politicians, in a softer light than I used to. I no longer see them as caricatures on the basis of their party affiliation or status, but as more vulnerable, more human, more genuine people. Gently turning towards a world I once scorned has given me a new perspective on it.

We may still be a long way from a truly mindful politics, society and world, but when powerful forces in our society start to take mindfulness seriously, alerted by hard evidence that the approach makes a difference, we are at least on the right road. Our capacity to journey skilfully along that road will depend on our ability and willingness to connect attentively and compassionately with the reality of the world as we find it, enquire into its needs and ask how we might fulfil them. This, of course, is the work of mindfulness practice itself.

Practice to try: Kindness meditation

Practising kindness is integral to all mindfulness meditations. By bringing an attitude of gentleness to our practice – whether in the patient returning of the mind to the breath, the allowing and holding of difficult emotions, or the willingness to open to the world around us rather than always trying to close down or manipulate – we cultivate a compassionate approach to life. We start to feel a connection with our minds and bodies, with others, and with the wider world. This sense of *kin*ship with all things is the root of *kind*ness, and once we have realised this connection, we naturally soften our approach. We can recognise that even when we have been treated unfairly, the most effective response is kindness. This doesn't mean tolerating injustice, putting up with abuse or failing to hold those who have mistreated us to account. Rather, it means taking action with everyone's best interests at heart.

Research suggests that practising kindness is good for us,[22] so, irrespective of the positive effect on the recipient of our generosity, we will benefit from adopting this attitude ourselves. Relationships are also likely to improve when we approach them with kindness: other people's mistrust tends to dissolve when we refrain from meeting it with our own. As Abraham Lincoln once said: 'Do I not destroy my enemies when I make them my friends?'[23] Or as the Buddha put it: 'Hatred is never appeased through hatred in this world – it is appeased only by loving-kindness.'[24] This is not easy to practise, of course. All our patterns of closing down, lashing out, blaming and judging tend to resurface when we are in conflict. The more stressed we become, the more we are prone to bias.

It is therefore helpful to work on practices that explicitly train our ability to offer friendliness in difficult situations. This can be particularly valuable when we decide to extend our practice into the social realm. The kindness meditation is one way of extending our capacity for compassionate relationships, even with people or in circumstances that can be very challenging.

1. Find a place to sit and practise, and spend a few minutes in mindfulness meditation, working with the breath as the object of meditation.

2. Bring to mind a person (or, if you prefer, an animal) for whom you feel a sense of love. This could be a family member, a friend, a pet, or someone who has been particularly generous to you. Picture them in your mind's eye, and allow your heart to open to them, letting yourself feel what naturally arises. You may notice a sense of warmth, friendliness or gratitude, in which case offer this to the person in your mind. Let the feelings radiate from you to them, as if in a loving embrace. If no such feelings arise, simply say to them, silently in your mind: 'I wish you happiness, health and joy' or 'I appreciate what you

have done for me' or simply 'I love you.' Choose words that express warm, genuine sentiments. Stay with your experience for a while. If the mind wanders, you can come back by bringing attention to the breath for a few seconds, then return to the sense of connection with the loved one and/or repeat the words of kindness. Treat this practice as an experiment – there is no 'correct' experience, and you don't need to try to force sentiments that aren't present. Know that you can stop at any time you need to.

3. Imagine now that you are standing in front of yourself, in your mind's eye. Recognise yourself as a human being, living with a human mind and body in a challenging world, with all the joys and difficulties that human life brings. If feelings of warmth, tenderness or compassion arise, extend them outwards to embrace your imagined self. You might picture yourself receiving a big hug, being cared for and supported. Silently in your mind, say something like: 'May I be happy, peaceful and joyful.' Once again, choose words and phrases that express a genuine sense of warmth, love and good wishes. Stay with the experience for a few minutes. Some people find that the prospect of offering kindness to themselves stirs up self-critical thoughts or feelings or anger, disappointment or shame. Notice these without judging them, or yourself for having them. You might like to include these automatic reactions as part of the 'you' that could be offered love and acceptance. Return to mindfulness of breathing for a time whenever you need to do so.

4. Allow the image of yourself to dissolve, and now bring to mind a person you know but about whom you have no strong feelings (either for or against). This 'neutral' person might be an acquaintance at work or someone you see each

day but do not know well. Recognising them as a fellow
living being who must deal with all the challenges of life,
repeat the process of offering up any feelings of kindness,
warmth and goodwill, perhaps accompanied by some
words: 'May you be well, may you find what you need to be
happy, may you be healthy.'

5. If you feel able, now bring to mind someone with whom
   you have a difficult relationship. This person might have
   mistreated you or they might have behaved in a way
   that you thought was wrong. You might be in an ongoing
   conflict with them. (However, it's usually better not to
   choose someone you have great difficulty with, when
   first practising this meditation.) See them in front of
   you, a fellow living being with a mind and a body who
   is contending with the pressures of their environment.
   Imagine what it must be like to be them, with their
   personal history, current difficulties and patterns of
   thinking and feeling that make up their experience of life
   right now. Recognising the challenges they face and the
   wide variety of influences on their thoughts, feelings and
   behaviour (many of which they can do little or nothing
   about), offer this person any feelings of kinship or
   understanding that arise. Imagine saying to them, 'It must
   be difficult being in your shoes – may you have the strength
   to manage skilfully and learn from the challenges in your
   life' or simply 'May you find peace.'

6. You might continue the practice by bringing to mind
   groups of people (everyone in your town or workplace,
   for example), or perhaps extend your offering of kindness
   to the whole planet and everyone and everything within
   it. You might picture the stress and suffering of the world,

and silently say something like: 'May we find skilful ways of working with our problems, may we let go of harmful ways of living, may we find well-being together as a planet.' Stay present to any feelings that arise, and let your words be a gateway to connecting with sensations so that the practice is embodied, rather than based only in thinking.

7. As you get up from the formal practice, make an intention to remain compassionately in touch with yourself and your environment, and to relate to everything you encounter, as much as you are able, with interest, warmth and openness. Continue to notice what happens, coming back to presence whenever you realise that the mind has wandered.

CHAPTER TEN

Giving to it ...

Any deep training opens in direct proportion
to how much we give ourselves to it.

Jack Kornfield[1]

Heart thumping. Weak legs. Pressure at the nose. Fluttery gut. Yawning. Thoughts revolving like a tumble dryer drum: I need a break ... I must sort this out ... I need more time ... I'm still no good at managing myself ... why don't I learn ... everything's gone wrong again ... An impulse to push everything – and every-one – away. Heaviness. Irritation. Anxiety.

But also: letting breath flow, unimpeded, at a rate that's much slower than the racing heartbeat. Watching the spinning thoughts – allowing their chatter – without blocking or grasping, or believing that what they're saying is true. Noticing the sensations of churn in the belly, and feeling the pressure in the sinuses ebbing and flowing, moment to moment. Recognising the familiar urge either to run and hide or act to try to get rid of what I'm feeling. Instead, gently staying present to what's here, now. Offering steadiness, kindness, gentleness – 'This is okay, and it will pass.' Continuing with whatever does need to be done – looking after the children and taking care of business – while reminding myself to rest, find support and recuperate when I can. Going to bed early, asking for a hug, meditating, slowing down.

Fifteen years down the line, I'm still prone to periods of anxiety. Usually they come when I've forgotten to allow, connect and flow with sensations, and instead have fallen into a pattern of pushing and grasping, or running to escape from feelings. Maybe it's due to a project that's causing discomfort, and my head says I've got to finish it quickly, to get it over with, so I can feel better. Pressing to complete, I fixate on the 'end date' in my mind, which starts to seem like a threat as it nears. Or maybe I feel bad because something's not turned out the way I would have liked, and my mind is running through it over and over again.

There are no lions here, just the predators I've dreamed up for myself. If I slow down, stay present and gentle, things can change. As I notice what's happening within me, bringing awareness to body sensations, and to the hurtling mental proliferation, I create the possibility of stepping out from it. I can observe how my connection to the world has closed down. I can watch the panic, the snapping at others, the distraction. As soon as I see what's going on, I'm no longer caught. The automatic thoughts and feelings continue, for a while, urging me into old reactions. But I know that the messages they send are not helpful in this situation, and probably not even accurate. As I bring awareness to mind and body, in time they respond with relief and a seemingly natural, gradual restoration of balance.

The more I've practised this approach, the less I've struggled, and the better life has become. I don't always notice immediately when I'm reacting in a way that exacerbates stress, but it's several years since I was last stuck in self-perpetuating anguish, with hardly a clue as to why it's happening or what to do about it. Once I spot the patterns, I'm not so fused with them, which gives me a choice. I know it's possible to watch difficult sensations and thoughts in awareness, with interest, kindness and equanimity. I can move my attention from my head to my body, connecting to a full sensory palette that brings me into the rolling present, away from the rigid and removed realm of fixation and rumination. I can breathe, open, and allow what's here to flow through. I can let go, directing my attention to the tasks of the day. I might still feel pain, and have a head full of wayward thoughts, but I am more confident in letting it all be, knowing that discomfort isn't all of who I am, even when it feels overwhelming. On the occasional nights when the pounding and whirring keep me awake, I might meditate until dawn. In the midst of difficulty, I can usually make good decisions.

Before I started practising mindfulness, my episodes of depression were becoming longer and more frequent. The more often they came, the more I tried to battle against them, and the longer I stayed anxious. The longer the depressions lasted, the more I panicked, perpetuating the cycle further. I worried about them even when I felt well – I was starting to believe I was broken, defective, unable to cope with life. I associated ever more strongly with my judgements about the labels I'd made for myself – 'mentally ill', 'depressive', 'hysterical', 'bipolar'. When difficulties came, as they inevitably did, these labels became self-fulfilling.

Mindfulness isn't a cure for all of life's troubles. But there are enormous benefits to practising awareness, paying attention to the full range of sensation, and consciously uncoupling from the thoughts, feelings and habits of our so-called selves. The challenges that come with being alive still arrive on our doorstep, but awareness allows us to transform our relationship with them. Gradually, as we let go into an embodied, fluid presence, over and over again, life becomes workable, even when it's tough.

When I was grappling with 'depression', I couldn't imagine sustaining a steady relationship, a family, or a fulfilling vocation. I certainly never believed that joy could come from moving towards painful realities that I desperately wanted to be shot of. And yet, these shifts have come through a process of opening up to, allowing and embracing experiences such as loss, uncertainty, fear, sadness and anger. As soon as I stopped *needing* to feel better, I started to feel better.

Over recent years, the cycles of anxiety that used to endure for months or years now tend to visit for only days or weeks. I'm no longer so in thrall to them when they appear. My environment offers more support for mindfulness, so, when the difficulties come, I can tap into a capacity for working with them, not just within me but around me. Bathed in a loving space, the problems that afflict me drop away faster.

It's not easy to stop searching for quick, simple routes to happiness. It's not easy to stop trying to get everything right. It's not easy to stop straining and struggling. Yet, if we give ourselves deeply to mindfulness, situations can unfold quite differently, and sometimes unexpectedly. We can develop a deeper awareness of pleasure and of pain. We can connect with joy *and* sorrow. We can become more grounded, and more in touch with the unstoppable reality of change. We can open up to the wonders of the world and realise how little we know about it, and how little we control it.

When we connect compassionately to *everything* that is happening, we free ourselves from the habits of grasping, delusion and resistance that contribute so much to our suffering. When we let go of struggle, we discover that experience has a richness to it, even when it's uncomfortable. We see, hear, taste, smell and feel in ways that are impossible when we are stuck in our so-called selves, unconsciously identified with the incessant thoughts in our heads. Instead, with awareness of what's happening in us and around us, we can learn how to move through life more lightly, more smoothly, more graciously, and let life move through us. This means opening up to feelings we might once have viewed as undesirable. But by doing so, we save ourselves from the stress that grasping and avoidance bring. In the process, we become more alive, more awake.

Mainstream mindfulness training is often offered as a short course, lasting no more than a couple of months. This can be a good beginning, but greater freedom is likely to be attained on an ongoing journey. In virtually every way imaginable, the invitation to mindfulness challenges our prevailing fixations. We are invited to practise awareness in a world full of busy, distracted minds. We are invited to appreciate life more openly, embracing its difficulties when grasping for pleasure and avoiding pain are the standard reactions to stress. We are invited to tune into the senses in a world that's run by ideas. We are invited to accept insubstantiality and impermanence in a culture that resists change and death. And we are invited to foster compassionate relationships with everything and everyone on a planet that's rife with separation, struggle and strife. We struggle against all of these shifts. Aspects of our biology, psychology and culture conspire against mindfulness, reinforcing a fixated, delusional mode of seeing and being that causes a lot of hassle. With so much inertia in these forces, transformation is difficult. In our minds, bodies and the world, feedback loops keep us from presence.

Often, when leading workshops, I show a stock picture that frequently accompanies media articles on mindfulness – a conventionally beautiful and tanned young woman wearing pristine white yoga pants sits alone in the lotus posture. With eyes closed and a wide smile across her face, she appears to be in a state of perfect bliss. Consciously or not, new meditators often compare their practice with this kind of image. This usually induces critical self-judgement, with people wondering why they do not look or feel as good as the woman in the picture. Perhaps they feel sad, angry or bored, and such images give them a reason to beat themselves up because their own practice isn't measuring up to what seems to be expected.

Mindfulness presented as hype is unhelpful. It happens when we get stuck in ideas about what the approach *should* be doing for us, and forget to connect with it as a living experience. Tuning into this living experience with presence and kindness is the heart of mindfulness training – we connect with it when we offer our minds and bodies to the practice, and to life, with an awakened, compassionate awareness.

Practice is key. As with any other skill, mindfulness deepens through repeated exercise. Practice doesn't mean trying to get somewhere else. It's an immediate expression of our intention to be present, right now. If we want presence in our life, we have to embody it, over and over again, and make it our way of being. The practice of embodiment is built into meditation training – when we stay present to unpleasant as well as pleasant experiences and come to understand how both change, moment by moment, we shift our habits from avoidance to connection. We move into the flow of life. We become gentler, softer, kinder, and our actions start to reflect this. With practice, transformation happens.

For most of us, this is a gradual process. Although we express mindfulness every time we come back to presence, making this a way of life takes time and gentle effort. We need to train deeply because, for most of us, this approach is so different from our existing habits, and the world isn't ready to support it (yet!). The forces that drive us into a reactive mode are strong. Nevertheless, research into mindfulness courses shows that the practice affects minds, bodies and behaviour. We can learn to sense what's happening more authentically, become more present, respond more wisely. As our training deepens, it's helpful to connect with experienced teachers and communities of practice, meditate each day, go on retreat, and explore traditions that have practised mindfulness over thousands of years.

Practice and support help us to guard against distortion. With our pushy, fearful minds – in our pushy, fearful world – it's easy to start grasping at or hiding in mindfulness, looking for a quick fix. We might be tempted to emphasise the easier or more palatable aspects of the approach. Perhaps gazing at a sunset is more appealing than opening up to feelings of pain or loss. However, the most radical and transformative aspects of the training – and therefore greater liberation – will prove elusive unless we engage with awareness in *every* aspect of life, both difficult and easy.

According to the Buddhist tradition, suffering ebbs away when we practise its tried and trusted methods, which shift our minds and lives from ignorance to wisdom, from attachment to equanimity, and from desire and aggression to gentle presence. These days, we might say that mindfulness training invites us into well-being, and that contentment comes from letting go of unskilful habits of mind and behaviour while gently cultivating a kind, patient and courageous approach to life, lived in awareness. When we remember to offer *our* hearts into the heart of mindfulness, deeply and repeatedly, these practices can help us find more peace – both in the moment and over the long term. This is what I've found, at least so far.

References

Chapter One

1   W. James (1907) 'The energies of men', *Science* NS25(635), pp. 321–32, at http://psychclassics.yorku.ca/James/energies.htm
2   M. Proust (1923) *Remembrance of Things Past*, Wordsworth Editions, vol. 2, p. 657

Chapter Two

1   T. Merton (1970) *The Wisdom of the Desert*, New Directions, p. 11
2   D. Hume (1738–40) *A Treatise of Human Nature*, Book 1, part IV, section 6, at http://isites.harvard.edu/fs/docs/icb.topic565657.files/9/hume.pdf
3   Quoted in J. Kornfield (2014) *A Lamp in the Darkness, Illuminating the Path through Difficult Times*, chapter 8, p. 57
4   For instance, see I. Kirsch (2014) 'Antidepressants and the placebo effect', *Zeitschrift für Psychologie* 222(3), pp. 128–34, at http://www.ncbi.nlm.nih.gov/pmc/articles/PMC4172306/

Chapter Three

1   H.G. Wells (1919) *The Outline of History*, at http://www.forgottenbooks.com/readbook_text/The_Outline_of_History_Being_a_Plain_History_of_Life_and_Mankind_1000114672/307
2   J. Kabat-Zinn (2001) *Full Catastrophe Living: How to Cope with Stress, Pain and Illness Using Mindfulness Meditation*, Piatkus
3   There is a discussion of the origin of this quote at

http://pjthompson.dreamwidth.org/394541.html

4   Quoted in 'Different ways of laughing' (2007),
    Guernica, at https://www.guernicamag.com/interviews/
    different_ways_of_laughing_1/

5   For example, see J. Kabat-Zinn (1982) 'An outpatient program
    in behavioral medicine for chronic pain patients based on the
    practice of mindfulness meditation: theoretical considerations
    and preliminary results', *General Hospital Psychiatry* 4(1),
    pp. 33–47; and J. Kabat-Zinn et al. (1992) 'Effectiveness of a
    meditation-based stress reduction program in the treatment
    of anxiety disorders', *American Journal of Psychiatry* 149(7), pp.
    936–43

6   For more on this research, see E. Halliwell (2010) *Be Mindful*,
    Mental Health Foundation

Chapter Four

1   Quoted in J. Goldstein (1976) *The Experience of Insight: A Natural
    Unfolding*, Unity Press, p. 70

2   J. Fang (2014) 'People would rather experience an electric shock
    than be alone with their thoughts', at http://www.iflscience.com/
    brain/people-would-rather-experience-electric-shock-be-alone-
    their-thoughts

3   M.A. Killingsworth and D.T. Gilbert (2010) 'A wandering mind is
    an unhappy mind', *Science* 330(6006), p. 932

4   J. Daubenmier (2014) 'It's not what you think, it's how you relate
    to it: dispositional mindfulness moderates the relationship
    between psychological distress and the cortisol awakening
    response', *Psychoneuroendocrinology* 48, pp. 11–18

5   See S. Gable and J. Haidt (2005) 'What (and why) is positive
    psychology?', *Review of General Psychology* 9(2), pp. 103–10

6   R.F. Baumeister et al. (2001) 'Bad is stronger than good',
    Review of General Psychology 5(4), pp. 323–70

7   For example, see E. Lisitsa (2014) 'The positive per-
    spective, Dr Gottman's Magic Ratio', at http://www.
    gottmanblog.com/sound-relationship-house/2014/10/28/
    the-positive-perspective-dr-gottmans-magic-ratio

8   For a list of cognitive biases, see https://en.wikipedia.org/wiki/
    List_of_cognitive_biases

9   O. Sacks (1995) *An Anthropologist on Mars*, Picador, quoted at http://
    www.longwharf.org/molly-sweeney-oliver-sacks-and-visual-
    agnosia

10 Quoted in F. Didonna (2008) *A Clinical Handbook of Mindfulness*,
    Springer, p. 43

11 A version of this story was originally told by Paul Watzlawick
    and appears in *Stiehl/Over* (2012) 'The solution is hopeless, but not
    serious: the pursuit of unhappiness', at http://www.stiehlover.
    com/en/blog-en/if-the-solution-is-the-problem-the-pope-of-
    communication-paul-watzlawick/

12 M. Tartakovsky (2013) 'Top relapse triggers for depression
    and how to prevent them', at http://psychcentral.com/lib/
    top-relapse-triggers-for-depression-how-to-prevent-them/

13 For example, see A. Chiesa et al. (2011) 'Does mindfulness
    training improve cognitive abilities? A systematic review of
    neuropsychological findings', *Clinical Psychology Review* 31(3), pp.
    449–64

14 J. Greenberg et al. (2012) '"Mind the trap": mindfulness practice
    reduces cognitive rigidity', *PLOS One*, at http://journals.plos.org/
    plosone/article?id=10.1371/journal.pone.0036206

15 For example, see https://en.wikipedia.org/wiki/
    Default_mode_network

16 J.A. Brewer et al. (2011) 'Meditation experience is associated with
    differences in default mode network activity and connectivity',
    *Proceedings of the National Academy of Sciences of the United States of
    America* 108(50), pp. 20254–9

17 For example, see B.K. Hölzel et al. (2011) 'How does mindful-
    ness meditation work? Proposing mechanisms of action from a
    conceptual and neural perspective', *Perspectives on Psychological
    Science* 6(6), pp. 537–59

18 J.A. Brewer et al. (2011) 'Meditation experience is associated with
    differences in default mode network activity and connectivity',
    *Proceedings of the National Academy of Sciences of the United States of
    America* 108(50), pp. 20254–9

19 P. Hai (2014) 'From walking: meditation in motion', at http://
www.lionsroar.com/walking-meditation-in-motion-your-guide-
to-buddhist-meditationjuly-2014/

20 J. Daubenmier (2014) 'It's not what you think, it's how you relate
to it: dispositional mindfulness moderates the relationship
between psychological distress and the cortisol awakening
response', *Psychoneuroendocrinology* 48, pp. 11–18

Chapter Five

1   From Dorothy Hunt, 'Peace is this moment without judgement',
at http://www.dorothyhunt.org/poetry_page.htm

2   For more on the effects of stress, see, for example, R. Sapolsky
(2012) 'How to relieve stress', at http://greatergood.berkeley.
edu/article/item/how_to_relieve_stress. Robert Sapolsky also
discusses the physiological effects of stress at http://news.
stanford.edu/news/2007/march7/sapolskysr-030707.html

3   D.M. Wegner (1994) 'Ironic processes of mental control',
Psychological Review 101(1), pp. 34–52

4   S. Bowen et al. (2014) 'Relative efficacy of mindfulness-based
relapse prevention, standard relapse prevention, and treatment
as usual for substance use disorders: a randomized clinical trial',
JAMA Psychiatry 71(5), pp. 547–56

5   J.A. Brewer et al. (2011) 'Mindfulness training for smoking cessation: results from a randomized controlled trial', *Drug and Alcohol
Dependence* 119(1–2), pp. 72–80

6   For example, see N.A. Farb et al. (2012) 'The mindful brain
and emotion regulation in mood disorders', *Canadian Journal of
Psychiatry* 57(2), pp. 70–7

7   See F. Zeidan et al. (2012) 'Mindfulness meditation-related pain
relief: evidence for unique brain mechanisms in the regulation
of pain', *Neuroscience Letters* 520(2), pp. 165–73

8   J. Kabat-Zinn (1982) 'An outpatient program in behavioral
medicine for chronic pain patients based on the practice
of mindfulness meditation: theoretical considerations and
preliminary results', *General Hospital Psychiatry* 4(1), pp. 33–47;

and J. Kabat-Zinn et al. (1992) 'Effectiveness of a meditation-based stress reduction program in the treatment of anxiety disorders', *America Journal of Psychiatry* 149(7), pp. 936–43

9   R.K. Wallace et al. (1971) 'A wakeful hypometa-bolic physiologic state', *American Journal of Physiology* 221(3), at http://relaxationresponse.org/publications/AmJPhysiology1971AWakefulHypometabolicPhysiologicState_BensonWallace.pdf

10 For example, see B.K. Hölzel et al. (2011) 'How does mindfulness meditation work? Proposing mechanisms of action from a conceptual and neural perspective', *Perspectives on Psychological Science* 6(6), pp. 537–59

11 A.A. Taren (2015) 'Mindfulness meditation training alters stress-related amygdala resting state functional connectivity: a randomized controlled trial', *Social Cognitive and Affective Neuroscience*, at http://www.ncbi.nlm.nih.gov/pubmed/26048176

12 R.A. Razza (2015) 'Enhancing preschoolers' self-regulation through mindful yoga', *Journal of Child and Family Studies* 24(2), pp. 372–85

13 UCLA Newsroom (2012) 'That giant tarantula is terrifying, but I'll touch it', at http://newsroom.ucla.edu/releases/that-giant-tarantula-is-terrifying-238055

14 M.A. Killingsworth and D.T. Gilbert (2010) 'A wandering mind is an unhappy mind', *Science* 330(6006), p. 932.

15 C.B. Parker (2015) 'Embracing stress is more important than reducing stress, Stanford psychologist says', *Stanford Report*, at http://news.stanford.edu/news/2015/may/stress-embrace-mcgonigal-050715.html

Chapter Six

1   From Dogen's Genjokoan as quoted at https://en.wikipedia.org/wiki/D%C5%8Dgen

2   For example, see R. Anderson (2000) *Being Upright: Zen Meditation and the Bodhisattva Precepts*, Rodmell, p. 119

3   See A. Olendzki, *Handle with Care, Cultivating Equanimity: The Mindfulness Wedge*, at http://sgforums.com/forums/1728/topics/486665

4   M. Kabat-Zinn and J. Kabat-Zinn (2014) *Everyday Blessings: Mindfulness for Parents*, Piatkus, p. 131

5   For example, see N. Wade (2005) 'Your body is younger than you think', *New York Times*, at http://www.nytimes.com/2005/08/02/science/your-body-is-younger-than-you-think.html?_r=0

6   BBC News (2000) 'Taxi drivers' brains "grow" on the job', at http://news.bbc.co.uk/1/hi/677048.stm

7   For example, see T.F. Münte et al. (2002) 'The musician's brain as a model of neuroplasticity', *Nature Reviews Neuroscience* 3, pp. 473–8

8   B. Draganski et al. (2004) 'Neuroplasticity: changes in grey matter induced by training', *Nature* 427, pp. 311–12

9   For example, see 'The split brain experiments', at http://www.nobelprize.org/educational/medicine/split-brain/background.html; further discussion in S. Harris (2015) *Waking up: Searching for Spirituality without Religion*, Black Swan

10 Quoted in J. Kornfield (2015) *Identification with Self*, at http://www.jackkornfield.com/identification-self/.

11 See ibid.

12 D. Wegner (2008) 'Self is magic', chapter prepared for J. Baer et al. (eds) *Psychology and Free Will*, Oxford University Press, at http://isites.harvard.edu/fs/docs/icb.topic67047.files/2_13_07_Wegner.pdf

13 I heard this description during Gay Watson's talk at the Play's the Thing Conference, London, 22/23 November 2011

14 B. Fuller (1970) *I Seem to Be a Verb*, Bantam

15 J.H. Fowler and N.A. Christakis (2009) *Connected: The Surprising Power of Our Social Networks and How They Shape Our Lives*, Little, Brown

16 J.A. Bargh et al. (1996) 'Automaticity of social behavior: direct effects of trait construct and stereotype activation on action', *Journal of Personality and Social Psychology* 71(2), pp. 230–44

17 See E. Langer (2009) *CounterClockwise: Mindful Health and the Power of Possibility*, Ballantine

18 Quoted in B. Hood (2012) *The Self Illusion: Why There is No 'You' Inside Your Head*, Constable, p. 34

19 B. Spinoza (1677) *The Ethics*, Part 2: *On the Nature and Origin of the*

Mind, at https://ebooks.adelaide.edu.au/s/spinoza/benedict/ethics/chapter2.html

20 See J. Kornfield (2008) *A Path with Heart: The Classic Guide through the Perils and Promises of Spiritual Life*, Bantam, p. 327

21 S. Batchelor (2011) *Confession of a Buddhist Atheist*, Spiegel and Grau, p. 131

22 N.A. Farb et al. (2007) 'Attending to the present: mindfulness meditation reveals distinct neural modes of self-reference', *Social Cognitive and Affective Neuroscience* 2(4), pp. 313–22

23 See Buddhadharma (2013) *A Questioning Life*, at http://www.lionsroar.com/a-questioning-life/

24 W.W. Wei (1963) *Ask the Awakened: The Negative Way*, Sentient, p. 7

25 Quoted in R. Hanson (2011) *Just One Thing: Developing a Buddha Brain, One Simple Practice at a Time*, New Harbinger p. 213

26 Quoted in Wildmind, at http://www.wildmind.org/blogs/on-practice/let-everything-happen-to-you

Chapter Seven

1 *The Matrix* (1999), at https://www.youtube.com/watch?v=6a3g8pFc0rg

2 R. Hind (2015) 'Vertical time: where mindfulness and music meet', *Guardian*, at http://www.theguardian.com/music/2015/sep/28/lost-in-thought-mindfulness-opera-st-lukes-london

3 Quoted in O. Burkeman (2014) 'Just sit down and think', *Guardian*, at http://www.theguardian.com/lifeandstyle/2014/jul/19/change-your-life-sit-down-and-think

4 Quoted in P. Young-Eisendrath (2008) *The Self-Esteem Trap: Raising Confident and Compassionate Kids in an Age of Self-importance*, Little, Brown

5 Quoted at http://peaceloveyoga.blogspot.co.uk/2012/01/one-you-are-looking-for.html

6 *This Is Spinal Tap* (1984), script at http://www.awesomefilm.com/script/thisisspinaltap.txt

7 At http://www.condenaststore.com/-sp/It-says-Someday-you-will-die-New-Yorker-Cartoon-Prints_i8481190_.htm

8 F. Kafka (1917–19) *The Blue Octavo Notebooks*, at

https://docs.google.com/document/d/1gD981HZ190BUJF-3czZNX3DsFWvqp3cq-Z4QS4d-9gw/edit?hl=en

9 J. Kabat-Zinn (2005) *Coming to Our Senses: Healing Ourselves and the World through Mindfulness*, Hyperion, quoted at http://link.springer.com/article/10.1007%2Fs12671-014-0307-1#/page-1

10 From *The Dhammapada*, quoted at http://www.floweringofgoodness.org/dhammapada.php

11 A. Frias et al. (2011) 'Death and gratitude: death reflection enhances gratitude', *Journal of Positive Psychology* 6(2), pp. 154–62

12 O. Burkeman (2012) 'How to harness the positive power of negative thinking', at http://greatergood.berkeley.edu/article/item/how_to_harness_the_power_of_negative_thinking

13 *Seinfeld* (1992), at https://www.youtube.com/watch?v=vnqBAuehmhM

14 For example, see J. Marsh and J. Sutie (2014) 'Is a happy life different from a meaningful one?', at http://greatergood.berkeley.edu/article/item/happy_life_different_from_meaningful_life

15 For example, see http://spot.colorado.edu/~chernus/NonviolenceBook/ThichNhatHanh.htm

16 For example, see 'Your breath and Julius Caesar's', at http://www.fromquarkstoquasars.com/estimating-how-many-molecules-you-breathe-that-were-from-julius-caesars-last-breath/

17 B. Bryson (2004) *A Short History of Nearly Everything*, Black Swan, p. 176

18 Accessed at http://allpoetry.com/Out-Beyond-Ideas

19 From W. Blake, 'The Marriage of Heaven and Hell', at http://www.blakearchive.org/exist/blake/archive/transcription.xq?objectid=mhh.c.illbk.14

20 J.E. Stellar et al. (2015) 'Positive affect and markers of inflammation: discrete positive emotions predict lower levels of inflammatory cytokines', *Emotion* 15(2), pp. 129–33

21 See R. Hanson, 'When good is stronger than bad', at https://www.rickhanson.net/teaching/tgc-public-summary/

22 A. Ginsberg (1966) 'Letter to the *Wall Street Journal*', at http://www.tricycle.com/special-section/letter-wall-street-journal-1966

23 T.N. Hanh (2015) 'Thich Nhat Hanh on the practice of mindfulness', at http://www.lionsroar.com/mindful-living-thich-nhat-hanh-on-the-practice-of-mindfulness-march-2010/

24   From W. Blake, 'The Marriage of Heaven and Hell', at
     http://www.blakearchive.org/exist/blake/archive/transcription.
     xq?objectid=mhh.c.illbk.14

Chapter Eight

1   R.M. Rilke, 'How Surely Gravity's Law', in *Book of Hours:
    Love Poems to God*, at http://consciousmovements.com/
    how-surely-gravitys-law/

2   Quoted in D. Loy (2008) *Money, Sex, War, Karma: Notes for a Buddhist
    Revolution*, Wisdom, p. i

3   S. Bridle, 'Comprehensive compassion: an interview with Brian
    Swimme', *What Is Enlightenment?*, at http://www.thegreatstory.org/
    SwimmeWIE.pdf

4   V. Frankl (2004) *Man's Search for Meaning*, Rider, pp. 12–13

5   L. Tzu, 'Always we hope', at http://truevoices.com/tag/lao-tzu/

6   A. Alter (2014) 'The powerlessness of positive thinking', *New
    Yorker*, at http://www.newyorker.com/business/currency/
    the-powerlessness-of-positive-thinking

7   See https://en.wikipedia.org/wiki/Ironic_process_theory

8   M. Marsh and D. Ketner (2015) 'How gratitude beats
    materialism', at http://greatergood.berkeley.edu/article/item/
    materialism_gratitude_happiness

9   E.W. Dunn et al. (2008) 'Spending money on others promotes
    happiness', *Science* 319(5870), pp. 1687–8

10   M. Marsh and D. Ketner (2015) 'How gratitude beats
     materialism', at http://greatergood.berkeley.edu/article/item/
     materialism_gratitude_happiness

11   'Sometimes I say that the buddhas and bodhisattvas are the
     most selfish of all. Why? Because by cultivating altruism they
     achieve ultimate happiness', at http://blog.gaiam.com/quotes/
     authors/dalai-lama/46295

12   For example, see I. Sample (2014) 'Loneliness twice as unhealthy
     as obesity for older people, study finds', *Guardian*, at http://
     www.theguardian.com/science/2014/feb/16/loneliness-twice-
     as-unhealthy-as-obesity-older-people; and R. Alleyne (2009)
     'Loneliness as harmful as smoking and obesity, say scientists',

Daily Telegraph, at http://www.telegraph.co.uk/news/health/
news/4636683/Loneliness-as-harmful-as-smoking-and-obesity-say-
scientists.html

13 The origin of this quote is discussed at http://quoteinvestigator.
com/2010/06/29/be-kind/

14 From the *Sedaka Sutta*, at http://www.accesstoinsight.org/tipitaka/
sn/sn47/sn47.019.olen.html

15 P. Condon et al. (2013) 'Meditation increases compassionate
responses to suffering', *Psychological Science* 24(10), pp. 2125–7

16 J.M. Darley and D. Batson (1973) 'From Jerusalem to Jericho:
a study of situational and dispositional variables in helping
behavior', *Journal of Personality and Social Psychology* 27(1), pp. 100–8

17 For example, see D. Keltner (2004) 'The compassionate instinct',
at http://greatergood.berkeley.edu/article/item/the_compassion-
ate_instinct; and Seppälä (2013) 'Compassion: our first instinct',
at https://www.psychologytoday.com/blog/feeling-it/201306/
compassion-our-first-instinct

18 Seppälä (2013) 'Compassionate mind, healthy body',
at http://greatergood.berkeley.edu/article/item/
compassionate_mind_healthy_body

Chapter Nine

1 Mindfulness All-Party Parliamentary Group (2015) *Mindful
Nation UK*, full report, at http://www.oxfordmindfulness.org/
wp-content/uploads/mindfulness-appg-report_mindful-nation-
uk_oct2015-002.pdf

2 J. Heaversedge and E. Halliwell (2012) *The Mindful Manifesto*, Hay
House, p. 195

3 J.R. Raphael, 'We're all data fatties, study finds', at
http://www.techhive.com/article/184244/Were_All_Data_
Fatties_Study_Finds.html

4 BBC News (2009) 'Depression looms as global crisis', at
http://news.bbc.co.uk/1/hi/8230549.stm

5 B. Khoury et al. (2013) 'Mindfulness-based therapy: a
comprehensive meta-analysis', *Clinical Psychology Review* 33, pp.
763–71

6　J.M.G. Williams and W. Kuyken (2012) 'Mindfulness-based cognitive therapy: a promising new approach to preventing depressive relapse', *British Journal of Psychiatry* 200(5), pp. 359–60

7　See Mindfulness All-Party Parliamentary Group (2015) *Mindful Nation UK*, full report, at http://www.oxfordmindfulness.org/wp-content/uploads/mindfulness-appg-report_mindful-nation-uk_oct2015-002.pdf

8　J.D. Creswell et al. (2012) 'Mindfulness-based stress reduction training reduces loneliness and pro-inflammatory gene expression in older adults: a small randomized controlled trial', *Brain, Behavior, and Immunity* 26(7), pp. 1095–101

9　See Mindfulness All-Party Parliamentary Group (2015) *Mindful Nation UK*, full report, at http://www.oxfordmindfulness.org/wp-content/uploads/mindfulness-appg-report_mindful-nation-uk_oct2015-002.pdf

10　X. Liu (2013) 'Can inner peace be improved by mindfulness training: a randomized controlled trial', *Stress and Health*, at http://www.oxfordmindfulness.org/wp-content/uploads/can-inner-peace-be-improved-by-mindfulness-training-a-randomized-controlled-trial.pdf

11　D.M. Levy et al. (2012) 'The effects of mindfulness meditation training on multitasking in a high-stress information environment', at https://faculty.washington.edu/wobbrock/pubs/gi-12.02.pdf

12　See Mindfulness All-Party Parliamentary Group (2015) *Mindful Nation UK*, full report, at http://www.oxfordmindfulness.org/wp-content/uploads/mindfulness-appg-report_mindful-nation-uk_oct2015-002.pdf

13　For example, see M.S. Krasner et al. (2009) 'Association of an educational program in mindful communication with burnout, empathy, and attitudes among primary care physicians', *Journal of the American Medical Association* 302(12), pp. 1284–93; and P.W. Chen (2013) 'Easing doctor burnout with mindfulness', *New York Times*, at http://well.blogs.nytimes.com/2013/09/26/easing-doctor-burnout-with-mindfulness/?_r=2

14　For an overview of mindfulness training for young people, see Mindfulness All-Party Parliamentary Group (2015) *Mindful*

Nation UK, full report, at http://www.oxfordmindfulness.org/wp-content/uploads/mindfulness-appg-report_mindful-nation-uk_oct2015-002.pdf

15 Ibid.

16 Ibid.

17 Mindfulness All-Party Parliamentary Group (2015) *Mindful Nation UK*, interim report, at http://www.themindfulnessinitiative.org.uk/images/reports/Mindful-Nation-UK-Interim-Report-of-the-Mindfulness-All-Party-Parliamentary-Group-January-2015.pdf

18 Ibid.

19 J.H. Fowler and N.A. Christakis (2009) *Connected: The Surprising Power of Our Social Networks and How They Shape Our Lives*, Little, Brown

20 J. Matthias (2014) 'Leading mindfully: two studies of the influence of supervisor trait mindfulness on employee well-being and performance', *Mindfulness* 5(1), p. 35, at http://ink.library.smu.edu.sg/cgi/viewcontent.cgi?article=4319&context=lkcsb_research

21 P. Chödrön (2001) *Start Where You Are: A Guide to Compassionate Living*, Shambhala Publications

22 For a summary, see 'Kindness research', Random Acts of Kindness Foundation, at https://www.randomactsofkindness.org/kindness-research

23 See https://en.wikiquote.org/wiki/Abraham_Lincoln

24 *The Dhammapada*, verse 5, at http://www.tipitaka.net/tipitaka/dhp/verseload.php?verse=005

Chapter Ten

1 J. Kornfield (2008) *A Path with Heart: The Classic Guide through the Perils and Promises of Spiritual Life*, Bantam, p. 57

Resources

With the mainstreaming of mindfulness has come a rapid and vast expansion of resources available to help you along your way. Here are a few suggestions for support you can access.

Mindfulness Courses

The gold standard mindfulness course remains the eight-week Mindfulness-Based Stress-Reduction (MBSR) course, as developed by Jon Kabat-Zinn. Addressing some of the core causes and manifestations of human stress and suffering, and offering a way to well-being in the midst of them, the course is appropriate for a wide range of situations and conditions. In the UK, MBSR courses can be found on the Be Mindful website (www.bemindful.co.uk) or via a Google search of your local area. Do check out the background and training of the person teaching the course – there is currently no accreditation for mindfulness teachers, although there is now a professional register supported by the major teacher training institutions – please see https://www.mindfulness-network.org/listingspagenew. php at the website of the UK Network for Mindfulness-Based Teacher Training Organisations.

There are a number of other mindfulness courses based on MBSR, the best known and researched of which is Mindfulness-Based Cognitive Therapy (MBCT), which was originally designed for people at greatest risk of depression, although it is now offered more widely. There are many others, such as Mindfulness-Based

Relapse Prevention (MBRP), and Mindfulness-Based Relationship Enhancement (MBRE), which take the MBSR course structure as their core, making minor adaptations for particular circumstances. If in doubt, MBSR is usually a good starting point, as it is suitable for most people in most circumstances.

Introductory workshops and taster sessions can also be helpful, as a way of getting to know the approach and the style of a particular teacher. Inevitably, the degree of insight and transformation that can be gained from a course is dependent on factors such as its length, the degree of investment requested and made by participants, and the experience of the teacher.

Some mindfulness teachers offer ongoing training beyond an eight-week course in the form of follow-up practice sessions, study and inquiry based on the main themes of the training.

If you are based in the south-east of England, I offer introductory days, mindfulness-based stress reduction courses, and practice sessions and retreat days for mindfulness course graduates in Sussex – see mindfulnesssussex.co.uk and mindfulnessretreats.co.uk for more details. I also offer mindfulness courses at the School of Life in Central London – please see mindfulnesslondon.co.uk for more details. I also offer workplace training and education in mindfulness – please contact me at edhalliwell.com if you are interested in bringing mindfulness to your organisation.

If you are inspired by the Buddhist tradition, there are many courses run by Buddhist organisations which present mindfulness in this context. Much of my early training and learning was at the London Shambhala Meditation Centre (www.shambhala.org.uk).

Mindfulness Retreats

Learning and practising mindfulness in a retreat setting is a good way of allowing time and space for your practice to deepen. I lived and worked at Dechen Choling in central France for a year, and it is possible to attend retreats at this Buddhist centre (as well as many others) ranging from a few days to much longer (www.dechencholing.org).

There is a growing range of opportunities for retreat practice with a mainstream mindfulness framework: Mindfulness Network CIC was set up by some of the main mindfulness UK teacher training institutes to offer retreats to the general public, ranging from one to seven days – see https://www.mindfulness-network.org/retreats.php. Retreats that I lead can be found at www.mindfulnessretreats.co.uk.

Mindfulness Online

Where possible, I would recommend learning mindfulness face-to-face, in a group, with an experienced teacher. However, sometimes this isn't possible, and there is a range of resources for people who can't get to a group, or as an additional support. Here are a few pointers:

www.bemindfulonline.com: A four-week introductory mindfulness course, co-led by myself and Tessa Watt, hosted by the Mental Health Foundation. It includes audio downloads, video guidance and email reminders.

www.mindful.org: Online content from the team behind *Mindful* magazine. News, features, practice guidance and blogs, including my regular contributions.

www.edhalliwell.com: My website, which includes more information on and links to my writing and other work, as well as audio downloads guiding you through many of the meditation practices from this book. You can also sign up to my mailing list here.

Twitter/Facebook

You can connect to the mindfulness and meditation world through some key Twitter accounts. Good starting points are @mindfulonline @greatergoodsc @_wildmind @jackkornfield @tricyclemag and @lionsroar. I tweet from @edhalliwell and post mindfulness news, quotes, poems and other links most days. For those interested in mindfulness in politics, you can find the Mindfulness Initiative @mindfulnationUK. I also have a Facebook page, which is at https://www.facebook.com/Ed-Halliwell-844596498899760/?ref=hl

Further Reading

There is a vast range of mindfulness-related books now available. Here are a few suggestions.

Pema Chödrön, *When Things Fall Apart: Heart Advice For Difficult Times* (Shambhala Publications, 1997). I would recommend any and all of Pema Chödrön's books, which present meditation from a Buddhist perspective, in a way that is accessible for all.

Ed Halliwell, *Mindfulness: How to Live Well By Paying Attention* (Hay House Basics 2015). A practical guide to bringing mindfulness to your life, with guidance for beginners and more experienced meditators. You could also try Jonty Heaversedge and Ed Halliwell, *The Mindful Manifesto: How Doing Less and Noticing More Can Help Us Thrive in a Stressed-Out World* (Hay House 2012), which was my first book, and sets out the case for mindfulness as a vital practice in the 21st century.

Jon Kabat-Zinn, *Full Catastrophe Living: How to Cope With Stress, Pain and Illness Using Mindfulness Meditation* (Piatkus, 2013). Jon Kabat-Zinn developed the mindfulness-based stress reduction course and is the pioneer in bringing mindfulness into mainstream settings. This book sets out the MBSR programme at length. I would also highly recommend his *Wherever You Go, There You*

Are: Mindfulness Meditation in Everyday Life (Hyperion, 1994), and the accompanying audio CDs to his books, which are available from http://www.mindfulnesscds.com/

Jack Kornfield, *A Path With Heart: A Guide Through the Perils and Promises of Spiritual Life* (Bantam, 1993). Jack Kornfield has devoted his life to bringing Eastern wisdom to the West and presenting it in depth, and in an accessible form. I would recommend any of his books.

Larry Rosenberg, *Breath by Breath, The Liberating Practice of Insight Meditation* (Shambhala Classics, 2004). An excellent, straight-forward guide to mindfulness foundations from a Buddhist perspective.

Chade-Meng Tan, *Search Inside Yourself: The Unexpected Path to Achieving Success, Happiness (and World Peace),* (Harper Collins, 2013). A lively and straight-talking course book for the workplace mindful-ness programme developed at Google.

B. Alan Wallace, *Minding Closely: The Four Applications of Mindfulness* (Snow Lion, 2011). A brilliant and in-depth exploration of mindfulness, also from a Buddhist perspective, by a foremost scholar, practitioner and scientist.

Mark Williams and Danny Penman, *Mindfulness: A Practical Guide to Finding Peace in a Frantic World* (Piatkus, 2011). Mark Williams is one of the developers of the MBCT course, and here sets it out for a general audience. It comes with a practice CD led by Mark.

Vidyamala Burch and Danny Peman, *Mindfulness for Health: A Practical Guide to Relieving Pain, Reducing Stress and Restoring Wellbeing* (Piatkus, 2013). Vidyamala is one of the leading developers of mindfulness programmes for pain management – you can find out more about her work at www.breathworks-mindfulness.org.uk

Index

Acknowledgements

This book was written in a small room alone, but it has only come to fruition thanks to the remarkable contributions and support of many people.

First, to all those who have taught me meditation, mindfulness and a path to saner living, I am hugely thankful. These include the generous, genuine and 'basically good' people at the London Shambhala Meditation Centre, who first took me in as a panicking twenty-something and taught me how to watch my breath and my mind, and supported me as I learned, stumbling, how to ride the mental and emotional storms that engulfed me. Also everyone at the Dechen Choling retreat centre in France, where sitting still for a month truly showed me that life could be seen and worked with differently, and where practising being present for a year gave me the nurturance needed to find a way of life that met my heart's longing. To Sakyong Mipham Rinpoche and everyone in Shambhala, thank you for helping and holding me ...

Thank you also to those in the mainstream mindfulness world who have taught and inspired me. To my supervisor Karunavira for your calm, steady, gentle presence, and to all those who have taught me how to teach mindfulness-based courses – especially Becca Crane, Jody Mardula, Michael Chaskalson, Pamela Erdmann and Cindy Cooper, as well as those who provided inspiration to start and continue along the teaching path, particularly Tessa Watt and Debbie Johnson.

It's been a pleasure to have worked alongside some wonderful and talented people at the Mindfulness Initiative, from whom I've learned much about taking mindfulness into the world of politics. Great appreciation goes to Madeleine Bunting, who was the driving force behind the Mindful Nation UK report, to Chris Cullen, who has been the principal teacher of mindfulness in the UK Parliament, to Willem Kuyken and Becca Crane who have generously devoted their time and resources (as well as that of their organisations) to the Initiative, and to all of the amazing associates and advisors who have given their energy selflessly to the project. Thanks also to the politicians who were prepared to trust in something a bit unusual – above all Chris Ruane, Tracey Crouch and Lorely Burt, former co-chairs of the Mindfulness All-Party Parliamentary Group.

It has been an honour and privilege to work – albeit briefly – alongside Jon Kabat-Zinn, as our paths crossed through his patronship of The Mindfulness Initiative, through sharing a UK publisher in Piatkus books, and on a stage set by The School of Life in London. In envisaging and forging a path for mindfulness in modern society, Jon's influence on my life's course and on hundreds of thousands, if not now millions, of others, has been vast. A deep bow of gratitude to you, Jon.

I have also been influenced by a number of teachers from afar in time and/or space, mainly through reading their books or from contact online, or through the influence of their students or structures. Thank you from a distance especially to Chogyam Trungpa Rinpoche, Jack Kornfield, Pema Chödrön, Alan B. Wallace, Eckhart Tolle, Bodhipaksa, Rick Hanson, Thich Nhat Hanh and Ken Wilber.

I'm inspired every day by the courageous, curious, trusting and insightful people who come to learn mindfulness, at workshops and on courses and retreats that I lead. The energy and vitality you bring is energising and vitalising, and a large part of what makes teaching such a pleasure. This would be a lonely path – and an impossible job – without you. I'm also inspired by the great lineages of meditation practitioners over the centuries, who have worked on their own minds and helped to clarify the workings of consciousness, pointing their discoveries out to those of us who follow, and helping us navigate our own journeys. I also greatly appreciate the patient work of mindfulness researchers, whose passion, patience and discernment have enabled an evidence base for the practice of mindfulness to grow, giving us another important perspective on what helps, how and for whom ...

Gratitude also goes to the places and people who've offered me spaces to teach. In particular, the Old School in Cuckfield, West Sussex (who also offered me a room in which to write this book), The School of Life in London, and Claridge House in Surrey. Thanks also to the many organisations who've invited me in to teach or present on mindfulness in their workplaces.

The development, editing and publishing of this book has depended on many people. Thanks first to my agents at The Marsh Agency: firstly Steph Ebdon, who helped me find a publisher, and then Susie Nicklin, who has offered great support and feedback during its writing. Thanks also to Anne Lawrance, who, as my editor at Piatkus books, trusted in an outline and believed in it enough to commit to publishing, and also offered great guidance and support as I attempted to turn the outline into a manuscript. Thanks also to Jillian Stewart, Clara Diaz, Claudia Connal and Aimee Kitson, who have all helped steer the book to final publication and enabled people to hear about it. My appreciation also goes to Philip Parr, whose skilful copyediting trimmed and refined my draft in ways that have greatly improved it.

A life's course is influenced by everyone who comes into contact with it, directly and indirectly – appreciation thus goes to everyone I've had the fortune to connect with: thank you for giving me lessons I can learn from. My apologies to those of you who have been hurt by my mindlessness.

There are some people to whom I owe a great debt for their support, kindness and love. To my parents and brothers – Ivor, Jill, Nick, Julian and Jeremy Halliwell, who have always offered me unconditional loving acceptance, sometimes despite great provocation. Thank you for not giving up on me. The same goes for my very good friends James Lowen and Will Fuller – your support when I needed it most has not been forgotten. Many, many other people also offered human contact, support and encouragement when I was most desperate for it – from Samaritans helpline volunteers to fellow support group attendees to healthcare professionals and dharma brothers and sisters. To all of you, thank you for helping me keep going when I had lost heart, and for helping me find that heart once more. May all those touched by suffering experience such kindness.

This book and my life would not be as it is without the sustained and sustaining love of my wife Vicki – your steady, unselfish, compassionate holding of the space of our lives together is precious to me way beyond words, and was especially so when I was preoccupied with writing this book. Quite simply, it couldn't have happened without you, and I promise it won't happen again. Finally, endless love and gratitude goes to our two 'live-in Zen masters', Arthur and Barnaby, who teach us so much every day. It's a great joy and a precious privilege to practise growing up with you.